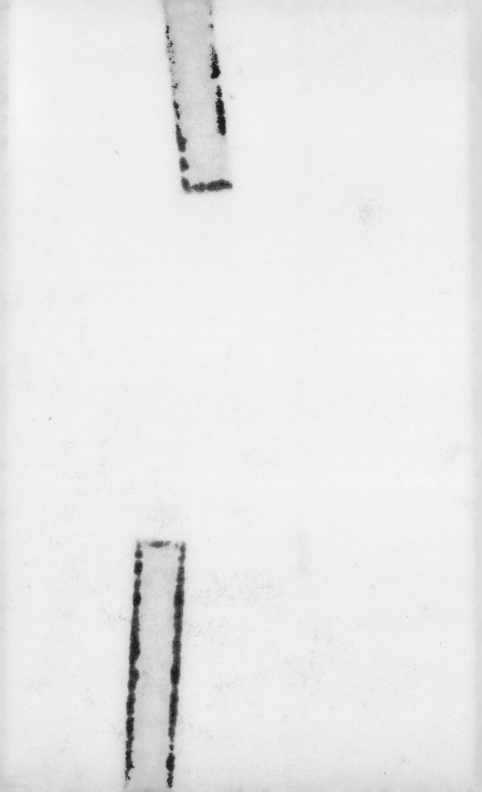

TO LIVE
IN PRONOUNS

PEDRO SALINAS

TO LIVE
IN PRONOUNS

Selected Love Poems

TRANSLATED BY

Edith Helman & Norma Farber

W · W · Norton & Company · Inc ·
New York 1974

Library of Congress Cataloging in Publication Data
Salinas, Pedro, 1892–1951.
To live in pronouns; selected love poems.
English and Spanish.
I. Helman, Edith Fistine, tr. II. Farber, Norma,
tr. III. Title.
PQ6635.A32T56   863'.6'2   74–5761
ISBN 0-393-04389-4
ISBN 0-393-04394-0 (pbk.)

This book was designed by Margaret F. Plympton.
Typeface used is Janson.
Manufacturing was done by Vail-Ballou Press, Inc.

PRINTED IN THE UNITED STATES OF AMERICA

1 2 3 4 5 6 7 8 9 0

CONTENTS

". . . true poetry places itself above events and though it may spring from them, it is superior to them and transports them to a place where contingencies are lost and only the pure essence remains."

PEDRO SALINAS

"In dynamic poetry, things are not what they are, they are what they become."

GASTON BACHELARD

"When a poem is written, it's finished, but it doesn't end; it begins, looks for another in itself, in the author, in the reader, in silence."

PEDRO SALINAS

"Each reader is another poet: each poem, another poem."

OCTAVIO PAZ

FOREWORD

The Spanish literary renaissance of the twentieth century is distinguished by the excellence of its lyric poets in successive generations to the present time. Early in the century, Unamuno, Antonio Machado, and Juan Ramón Jiménez, concerned with the discovery of authentic human values and new forms of expression, create inward poetry of deep self-scrutiny. In the same first decades, in various fields, the same concern and search animate the creative activity of such universal Spaniards as Ortega, Picasso, and Casals. Lorca's generation—or the generation of 1925, as it is often called—begins to publish major works of poetry in a very special atmosphere, which Jorge Guillén, one of the greatest poets of our century, characterizes in a few words, at the same time epitomizing the attitude toward poetry of the whole generation: "To understand the atmosphere of those years, one must grasp this will to poetry as creation, this acceptance of the poem as the world in quintessence." The group includes Pedro Salinas and his close, lifelong friend Jorge Guillén, Gerardo Diego, Dámaso Alonso, García Lorca, Alberti, and Aleixandre, among others. They are held together by warm friendship, by the same way of feeling poetry in its widest connotation, and in their common literary heritage. They all know modern French poetry, its great innovations from Baudelaire and the symbolists through the surrealists. What is remarkable is that they manage to blend harmoniously the discoveries made by modern poets in Europe and America with all that they learn from their close study of Spanish poets of the past, for example, Garcilaso, Saint John of the Cross, and Gón-

3

gora, and from the traditional folk poetry of Spain as well. The poets of the generation of 1925, however, despite their common poetic heritage and criteria, write poetry that is very different in content and style. Each of the poets has his own distinctive voice, which, in the case of Salinas, is the same clear, unmistakable voice throughout his works, the essays, fiction, and drama he wrote, as well as in his nine books of poetry.

Salinas's poetic voice is his speaking voice. He reminds us that poetry used to be synonymous with telling, *decir:* The urgent desire to tell impels the poet to speak. In his essay in defense of language he observes that speaking is understanding and understanding is constructing oneself and the world. Speaking, moreover, postulates someone listening, hearing, reacting to what is being said: A monologue or dialogue is taking place. Even when the poet speaks to himself in the first person in a poem, he initiates us listeners-hearers-readers into his attitude toward reality, into his way of perceiving objects, not only their surface appearances but their deeper aspects as well. When he addresses things or creatures—a handful of sand on the beach or a harvest fly singing, a tree reflected in the pool or an image in the mirror, a child in his cradle or the poet's own shadow—he always reveals some unsuspected aspect of the object or some surprising reaction of his own toward it. His endless desire to penetrate what he perceives, to reach what is not seen, is the theme of a short poem titled aptly enough "To See What's Invisible" ("Mirar lo invisible"), in his second book, *Seguro azar* (*Certain Chance*), in which he says that it is not for what he can see that he keeps his eyes open, but rather, "For a world suspected/ concrete and virginal behind, / for what I cannot see, / I keep my eyes wide open." This yearning for what is back

4

of what his eyes perceive is in no way a rejection or renunciation of the experiences of the senses. On the contrary, Salinas has an insatiable curiosity about things and a natural power to wonder about them, to re-create them, enjoy them fully. He takes incomparable delight in surfaces, textures, appearances, everything his eye catches, in its restless roving, but then his mind's eye takes over and is impelled to pierce the crust of the "real," to reach what is essential behind or on the reverse side of the outer surface.

If in a poem he is addressing a person, perception follows the same course, the same process of seeking the deepest core of the person takes place. In an early poem, for example, from his first book, suggestively titled *Presagios* (*Foreshadowings*), in the poem simply numbered 8, when the beloved tells him that she loves him with all her soul, gives him her whole soul, the poet confesses to himself, ". . . in my heart / I feel an emptiness that only / will be filled by that soul / that you do not give me." He feels the irresistible longing to uncover the unknown self hidden behind the visible self that is speaking to him. Many of the later love poems are variations on this theme of probing to find or helping to create the better or higher self latent within the lover-poet and the beloved-interlocutor. The persistent questioning heightens the excitement of the drama of thir changing relationship, which the reader inevitably shares and he follows the interaction between the lovers, discovering with them that each of them becomes most authentically himself through his love for the other. The dialogue device actualizes the transformations they and their relationship undergo in moments that are always in the present time, the eternal present of lovers and of the poems that tell their life lived in pronouns.

To Live in Pronouns, the title of this collection, is taken from a line in the first stanza of a poem in *La voz a ti debida* (1933) (*The Voice Owed to You*). The stanza says, "To live my life I don't want / islands, palaces, towers. / What higher joy / to live in pronouns!" Why pronouns? In pronouns the lovers can live at the beginning of the world, before there were names, before time was measured or space charted. "You" and "I" are more essential, immediate, and intimate than given names. These pronouns are the protagonists in the three books of love poems, the first, *La voz a ti debida*, its sequel *Razón de amor* (1936) (*Love's Reason,* or *Reasoning*) and in the posthumously published *Largo lamento* (*Long Lament*) which includes poems written until 1938 but for the most part unpublished before the *Poesias completas* edition of 1971. The poems in this collection are selected mainly from the first two books and a few from the third; several earlier poems, analogous in feeling or thought to later poems are included as well and placed right after the poems they are thematically related to. The *indice de primeros versos* indicates the title of the book each poem comes from. The order in which the poems appear in the original books is not necessarily followed in this collection, which includes roughly a third of the love poems. The whole trilogy of the love poems was composed in the thirties but we do not know the dates of composition of the individual poems. Actually, Salinas published the first two volumes as single long poems, adding the subtitle *Poema* to *La voz a ti debida* and *Poesia* to *Razón de amor*. The individual, untitled poems, complete in themselves, are not arranged in any narrative or time sequence. The separate moments of love, in its very different moods, are enacted by the players, in the dialogue that re-creates them.

The first poem, in this collection and in *La voz a ti*

6

debida, begins with the pronoun "tú" and ends with the pronoun "yo," the "you" and "I" that enclose the magic world of the lovers. The Spanish "tú" is infinitely more intimate than English "you" and the feeling of intimacy is reinforced in Spanish by the corresponding familiar verb endings. The lovers are already established in their love relationship. They are friends as well as lovers and share equally the experience they are living. The poet-lover is telling the beloved what she is like as a person, her dynamism, "You live always in your actions." Her need for clarity, for certainty, "Only from your eyes / emanates the light / that guides your steps. You go / only by what you see . . ." ". . . You can't bear doubting." ". . . And you never made a mistake / except once, one night / when a shadow caught your fancy—/ the only one you've ever liked. / It seemed a shadow. / And you wished to embrace it. / And it was me." The personality of the beloved emerges as the poet discovers her in her usual way of being, of acting, of living. Until her own perilous mistake, which starts up the process of mutual transformation told by the poems. There are no adjectives used in this first poem describing her physical appearance; her eyes are mentioned because of the light they shed, but we do not know their color. There are very few concrete physical references in the rest of the poems, the rose color of her body, the palpable quality of her voice; her beauty is invoked or alluded to with some frequency and the adjective *alta* is used in its different connotations, so that it may mean "tall" but also suggests "exalted" or "sublime." For the most part the dialogue evokes the real presence—actual even in absence—of the person who is the beloved and also one of the two loving, in moments of transport or tenderness, of joyous fulfillment or of anguished questioning, of belief in the supreme reality of love and of doubt of its very existence. Wonderment never ceases, from the first encounter, a lightning-flash, a blinding illumination: "I found you suddenly, / in that brutal rending / of darkness and light, / where depths are revealed / that escape from day and night . . ." Salinas quotes Shelley's invocation from his "Epipsychidion," "Thou Wonder, and Thou Beauty, and Thou Terror" on the title page of *La voz a ti debida* because, no doubt, it epitomizes his own feelings as he evokes his own love and the young woman who inspired it. The past tense "found" is used here to indicate a single moment in the past when the happening took place. For the most part, the verbs are in the present tense, making each moment actual.

When fulfillment takes place, he has to dream it, so that if it is not true, or if he loses her, he will only have lost "a shadow, one dream more." The questioning of her existence, of her love, right from the beginning, acts as a kind of counterpoint to the joy of fulfillment. The movement of constant change creates tension and suspense that engage and hold the reader, who is also carried along by the rhythmic flow and the varying length of the lines. The length of line paces the action, feeling, or contemplation. Joyous fulfillment transforms the world and the lovers themselves but there is ever more to search for within their depths until they can achieve "Total love, as the love of mass for mass." Love is ceaseless aspiration upward, ascent toward the attainment of oneness that will enable each to live the other and each to be lived by the other: "What joy to live / feeling lived. / To yield / to the deep certainty, darkly, / that another creature, outside me, far away, / is living me." Through this love each achieves a new identity, a more authentic self: "And gradually, / you are forming yourself, / giving birth to yourself, / within your love, / my love, mingled, / as the day forms itself / within the great dark doubt." This new being of hers only the lover can perceive. Others see her apparent, superficial, light-hearted, laughing self. The deeper self, back of the apparent self, finds itself in the love "that I extend always / like a burning mirror." This deeper self that she discovers through their love, however, prevails only intermittently. The other self inevitably reappears and even threatens to destroy the newly found or created authentic self. Instants of rapture, when communication becomes communion, cannot endure. Living, says the poet, is leaving each other and love is only the miraculous postponement of its own ending. Exclamations of wonderment give way to questions: "Will you be, love, / a long never-ending good-by?" one poem begins. The leave-taking poems are among the most suggestive and original, along with those on the presence-in-absence theme. The anguish of separation is transmuted into joyous remembrance, reliving of the happy moments recaptured from the past and re-created in poems which overcome love's great enemy, time.

These poems so vividly recall moments in the love drama played by the two pronoun-protagonists that the reader may have the impression that they are moments actually experienced by them and merely reproduced by the poet. Salinas, is his critical essays, considers again and again the relation of poetry to life and concludes, "All poetry operates on one reality for the sake of creating another." Referring specifically to the erotic and love poetry of Rubén Darío, he doubts that biographical information about the poet is of much value to the literary critic or the readers who wish to understand and enjoy his poetry, explaining why: ". . . the job of the poet is not to reproduce that first experience, but to create another, the work, new, different, free in its new being. . . . The world of artistic forms is life, of course. But it's not this life. . . . It's another life. The musical score, painting, poem, are created by man over their material existences, precisely in order to rise above them, to transcend them in a fabulous operation of the imagination which is incomparably more than the simple double, copy or repetition, with which realistic theory led so many heads astray." To transcend material existence, as we have seen, is a constant goal in Salinas's poetry, penetrating surfaces, seeing the unseen, intuiting what is behind the loved one's apparent way of being. It is illuminating to examine his use of words beginning with the prefix *tras*, many of which he invents and which have no real equivalents in English, for example, *trasvisible, trasamor, trasluces de paraíso* ("glimmerings of paradise"). In Spanish, *tras* means not only "behind," "back of," but also "after," which makes possible *traspresencia* meaning "presence after separation" or "everlasting presence," a wonderfully evocative word in poems created out of remembrance.

Salinas borrows for his title *La voz a ti debida* words from a line in the third Eclogue by the great Renaissance poet Garcilaso. In commenting on Garcilaso's possible use of facts of reality in writing his love lyrics, Salinas observes that though the poems may begin with, be based on, realities of the world, they then unfold, are elaborated "in his [the poet's] consciousness, in his inner being, like a long drama, the first act or scenes of which have been seen by the public while the rest of it continues toward its end, far from any possible observation by people," an observation perfectly applicable to his own love poems. The only thing clear, he says, is that when the poet creates the beloved, he endows her with the best he can find in himself. Garcilaso's beloved, conceived within the pastoral tradition, is the object of a very different kind of love—unaccepted, unrequited—and the lover-poet is the adoring, submissive slave of the remote and inaccessible beloved. Nevertheless, when Salinas is preparing for publication his first book of love poems, it is in Garcilaso's poetry that he finds its marvelously ambiguous and evocative title, *La voz a ti debida* (*The Voice Owed to You*). The pronoun "you": the beloved or love itself? In Garcilaso's line, the words allude to the poet's voice, inspired by his love-muse, and he expresses the hope that it will survive the silencing of his physical voice. Salinas is well-aware of the full meaning and impact of Garcilaso's words when he chooses precisely those words for the title of his first book of love poems, a title that could be used as well for the whole trilogy. For in all these poems, Salinas's poetic voice, wonderfully expressive and alive, continues to tell us the joys, and the pain, of many different moments of love.

For those of us who knew Salinas, his poetic voice invariably recalls his physical voice, the voice we heard when he shared with each student his fervent love and deep understanding of the great works of literature, to which his voice gave new and enduring life. It's the voice we heard in his incomparable conversation, inexhaustibly imaginative, impassioned or humorous, always so stimulating that one felt more intensely alive talking with him. So many delightful anecdotes to be told but this is not the place to tell them.

ACKNOWLEDGMENTS

For permission to translate and publish these poems I am deeply indebted to the family of Pedro Salinas, his daughter Soledad Salinas de Marichal and to his son Jaime Salinas.

They generously granted me permission to select poems from the complete poetic work of their father. I thank them for all their kindness and consideration.

I wish to thank them also for allowing us to print the Spanish text of the poems as they appeared in the recent edition of the *Poesias completas* (Barcelona; Barral Editores, 1971) that was prepared by Soledad Salinas de Marichal.

I regret not to be able to list the names of all the editors of editions or anthologies and especially the authors of studies on Salinas's poetry, whom I have consulted and to whom I owe a great deal, most particularly to Jorge Guillén, Juan and Soledad Marichal, Cortázar, Feal Deibe, Alma de Zubizarreta, and many others. My own understanding of the poetry, my reading of the poems, would not have been possible without all the groundwork they had done before me and for me. My appreciation and thanks to them all.

Edith Helman

PART I

Tú vives siempre en tus actos.
Con la punta de tus dedos
pulsas el mundo, le arrancas
auroras, triunfos, colores,
alegrías: es tu música.
La vida es lo que tú tocas.

De tus ojos, sólo de ellos,
sale la luz que te guía
los pasos. Andas
por lo que ves. Nada más.

Y si una duda te hace
señas a diez mil kilómetros,
lo dejas todo, te arrojas
sobre proas, sobre alas,
estás ya allí; con los besos,
con los dientes la desgarras:
ya no es duda.
Tú nunca puedes dudar.

Porque has vuelto los misterios
del revés. Y tus enigmas,
lo que nunca entenderás,
son esas cosas tan claras:
la arena donde te tiendes,

You live always in your actions.
With the tips of your fingers
you explore the world, pulling out
dawns, triumphs, colors,
delights: it's your music.
Life is whatever you play.

Only from your eyes
emanates the light
that guides your steps. You go
only by what you see. No other way.

And if a doubt signals you
from ten thousand kilometers,
you leave everything, you rush out
on prows, on wings,
you're there already. With kisses,
with teeth you tear it to shreds:
nothing's left of doubt.
You can't bear doubting.

Because you've turned the mysteries
around. And your enigmas,
what you'll never understand,
are such clear things:
the sand where you stretch out,

la marcha de tu reló
y el tierno cuerpo rosado
que te encuentras en tu espejo
cada día al despertar,
y es el tuyo. Los prodigios
que están descifrados ya.

Y nunca te equivocaste,
más que una vez, una noche
que te encaprichó una sombra
—la única que te ha gustado—.
Una sombra parecía.
Y la quisiste abrazar.
Y era yo.

the ticking of your watch
and the delicate rose-tint body
you meet in your mirror
every day on waking,
and it's yours. Enigmas
that are already deciphered.

And you never made a mistake
except once, one night
when a shadow caught your fancy—
the only one you've ever liked.
It seemed a shadow.
And you wanted to embrace it.
And it was me.

No, no dejéis cerradas
las puertas de la noche,
del viento, del relámpago,
la de lo nunca visto.
Que estén abiertas siempre
ellas, las conocidas.
Y todas, las incógnitas,
las que dan
a los largos caminos
por trazar, en el aire,
a las rutas que están
buscándose su paso
con voluntad oscura
y aún no lo han encontrado
en puntos cardinales.
Poned señales altas,
maravillas, luceros;
que se vea muy bien
que es aquí, que está todo
queriendo recibirla.
Porque puede venir.
Hoy o mañana, o dentro
de mil años, o el día
penúltimo del mundo.
Y todo

No, don't keep closed
the doors of night,
of the wind, of lightning,
of what's never been seen.
Let them be open always,
all of them, the known ones
and the unknown,
those that open out
on the long roads
to be marked out, in the air,
on the routes that are
seeking their passage
with dark purpose
and haven't found it
on the cardinal points.
Put up high signals,
marvels, bright stars;
let it be seen clearly
that this is the place, that everything
is eager to receive her.
Because she may be coming.
Today or tomorrow, or within
a thousand years, or the day
before the end of the world.
And everything

tiene que estar tan llano
como la larga espera.

Aunque sé que es inútil.
Que es juego mío, todo,
el esperarla así
como a soplo o a brisa,
temiendo que tropiece.
Porque cuando ella venga
desatada, implacable,
para llegar a mí,
murallas, nombres, tiempos,
se quebrarían todos,
deshechos, traspasados
irresistiblemente
por el gran vendaval
de su amor, ya presencia.

must be as plain
as the long waiting.

Although I know it's pointless.
That it's all a game of mine,
waiting for her this way
as for a breath or a breeze,
afraid she may stumble.
Because when she comes,
wildly, relentlessly,
to reach my side:
walls, names, aeons
would all break asunder,
destroyed, pierced
irresistibly
by the windstorm
of her love, now an actual presence.

Ha sido, ocurrió, es verdad.
Fue en un día, fue una fecha
que le marca tiempo al tiempo.
Fue en un lugar que yo veo.
Sus pies pisaban el suelo
este que todos pisamos.
Su traje
se parecía a esos otros
que llevan otras mujeres.
Su reló
destejía calendarios,
sin olvidarse un hora:
como cuentan los demás.
Y aquello que ella me dijo
fue en un idioma del mundo,
con gramática e historia.
Tan de verdad,
que parecía mentira.

No.
Tengo que vivirlo dentro,
me lo tengo que soñar.
Quitar el color, el número,
el aliento todo fuego,
con que me quemó al decírmelo.
Convertir todo en acaso,

It happened, it really did take place.
It was on a day, it was a date
that brands time for all time.
It was in a place I can see.
Her feet were stepping on this very ground
we all do.
Her dress
looked like those others
that other women wear.
Her watch
unwove calendars,
without forgetting an hour:
counting as the rest do.
And what she said to me
was in a language of the world,
with grammar and history.
So real,
it seemed incredible.

No.
I have to live it inwardly,
I have to dream it for myself.
Remove the color, the number,
the breath all fire,
with which she burned me as she said it to me.
Convert everything to chance,

en azar puro, soñándolo.
Y así, cuando se desdiga
de lo que entonces me dijo,
no me morderá el dolor
de haber perdido una dicha
que yo tuve entre mis brazos,
igual que se tiene un cuerpo.
Creeré que fue soñado.
Que aquello, tan de verdad,
no tuvo cuerpo, ni nombre.
Que pierdo
una sombra, un sueño más.

to pure accident, dreaming it.
In that way, when she retracts
what she said to me then,
I won't be stung with grief
at having lost a happiness
I held in my arms,
as a body is held.
I'll believe it was dreamed.
That what was so real
had no body, no name.
That I'm losing
a shadow, one dream more.

¿Por qué tienes nombre tú,
día, miércoles?
¿Por qué tienes nombre tú,
tiempo, otoño?
Alegría, pena, siempre
¿por qué tenéis nombre: amor?

Si tú no tuvieras nombre,
yo no sabría qué era,
ni cómo, ni cuándo. Nada.

¿Sabe el mar cómo se llama,
que es el mar? ¿Saben los vientos
sus apellidos, del Sur
y del Norte, por encima
del puro soplo que son?

Si tú no tuvieras nombre,
todo sería primero,
inicial, todo inventado
por mí,
intacto hasta el beso mío.
Gozo, amor: delicia lenta
de gozar, de amar, sin nombre.

Why do you have a name:
day, Wednesday?
Why do you have a name:
time, autumn?
Joy, sorrow, everlastingly
why do you have a name: love?

If you had no name,
I wouldn't know what it was,
nor how, nor when. Nothing.

Does the sea know its name,
that it's the sea? Do the winds
know they're called South
and North, over and above
their sheer blowing?

If you had no name
everything would be primordial,
the beginning, all invented
by me,
untouched until my kiss.
Joy, love: unhurried delight
of enjoying, of loving, without a name.

Nombre: ¡qué puñal clavado
en medio de un pecho cándido
que sería nuestro siempre
si no fuese por su nombre!

Name: what a dagger driven
into an innocent breast
that would be ours forever
if not for its name!

Yo no necesito tiempo
para saber cómo eres:
conocerse es el relámpago.
¿Quién te va a ti a conocer
en lo que callas, o en esas
palabras con que lo callas?
El que te busque en la vida
que estás viviendo, no sabe
más que alusiones de ti,
pretextos donde te escondes.
Ir siguiéndote hacia atrás
en lo que tú has hecho, antes,
sumar acción con sonrisa,
años con nombres, será
ir perdiéndote. Yo no.
Te conocí en la tormenta.
Te conocí, repentina,
en ese desgarramiento brutal
de tiniebla y luz,
donde se revela el fondo
que escapa al día y la noche.
Te vi, me has visto, y ahora,
desnuda ya del equívoco,
de la historia, del pasado,
tú, amazona en la centella,
palpitante de recién

I don't need time
to know what you're like:
finding each other is a lightning-flash.
Who can get to know you
by what you don't say, or those
words with which you conceal it?
Anyone who looks for you in the life
you're living, knows
nothing but hints of you,
pretexts in which you hide.
Going in pursuit of you, backward
into what you've done, before,
adding action to smile,
years to names, will be
losing you. I won't.
I found you in the storm.
I found you, suddenly,
in that brutal rending
of darkness and light,
where depths are revealed
that escape from day and night.
I saw you, you've seen me, and now,
stripped bare of ambiguity,
of history, of the past,
you, amazon in the flash of fire,
panting from your recent

llegada sin esperarte,
eres tan antigua mía,
te conozco tan de tiempo,
que en tu amor cierro los ojos,
y camino sin errar,
a ciegas, sin pedir nada
a esa luz lenta y segura
con que se conocen letras
y formas y se echan cuentas
y se cree que se ve
quién eres tú, mi invisible.

unexpected arrival,
you've been mine from so long ago,
I've known you for such a long time,
I close my eyes in your love,
and walk without wavering,
blindly, without asking anything
of that slow sure light
by which letters are recognized,
and shapes, and accounts are kept
and people think they see
who you are, my invisible one.

¡Qué gran víspera el mundo!
No había nada hecho.
Ni materia, ni números,
ni astros, ni siglos, nada.
El carbón no era negro
ni la rosa era tierna.
Nada era nada, aún.
¡Qué inocencia creer
que fue el pasado de otros
y en otro tiempo, ya
irrevocable, siempre!
No, el pasado era nuestro:
no tenía ni nombre.
Podíamos llamarlo
a nuestro gusto: estrella,
colibrí, teorema,
en vez de así, "pasado";
quitarle su veneno.
Un gran viento soplaba
hacia nosotros minas,
continentes, motores.
¿Minas de qué? Vacías.
Estaban aguardando
nuestro primer deseo,
para ser en seguida
de cobre, de amapolas.

What a night, the night before the world!
Nothing had been made.
No substance, no numbers,
no stars, nor centuries, nothing.
Coal wasn't black,
and the rose wasn't delicate.
Nothing was anything, as yet.
How innocent to believe
that the past belonged to others
in another time, now
irrevocable, forever!
No, the past was ours:
it didn't even have a name.
We could call it
whatever we wished: star,
hummingbird, theorem,
instead of "the past."
We could remove its sting.
A strong wind
was blowing mines, continents,
motors toward us.
What kind of mines? Empty ones.
They were waiting
for our first wish,
so they'd at once become
copper, poppies.

Las ciudades, los puertos
flotaban sobre el mundo,
sin sitio todavía:
esperaban que tú
les dijeses: "Aquí",
para lanzar los barcos,
las máquinas, las fiestas.
Máquinas impacientes
de sin destino, aún;
porque harían la luz
si tú se lo mandabas,
o las noches de otoño
si las querías tú.
Los verbos, indecisos,
te miraban los ojos
como los perros fieles,
trémulos. Tu mandato
iba a marcarles ya
sus rumbos, sus acciones.
¿Subir? Se estremecía
su energía ignorante.
¿Sería ir hacia arriba
"subir"? ¿E ir hacia dónde
sería "descender"?
Con mensajes a antípodas,
a luceros, tu orden
iba a darles conciencia
súbita de su ser,
de volar o arrastrarse.
El gran mundo vacío,
sin empleo, delante
de ti estaba: su impulso
se lo darías tú.

Cities and harbors
were floating over the world,
still without location.
They were waiting
for you to tell them: "here"—
for launching boats,
machines, festivals.
Machines impatient
to have a destiny:
for they would generate light
if you ordered it,
or autumn nights
if you wanted them.
Verbs, undecided,
were looking you in the eye
like faithful dogs,
quivering. Your command
was going to designate
their directions, their actions.
To climb? Their unguided energy
trembled.
Would going up mean
"climbing"? And in what direction
would "descending" be?
With messages to the antipodes,
to the day-stars, your command
was going to give them
sudden awareness of their existing,
of their flying or their dragging along.
The great empty world,
without employment, was standing there
before you: you'd give it
its impulse.

Y junto a ti, vacante,
por nacer, anheloso,
con los ojos cerrados,
preparado ya el cuerpo
para el dolor y el beso,
con la sangre en su sitio,
yo, esperando
—ay, si no me mirabas—
a que tú me quisieses
y me dijeras: "Ya."

And close by you, undesignated,
breathless to be born,
with eyes shut,
with body quite prepared
for sorrow and kiss,
with blood circulating:
there I was, waiting—
o what if you didn't look at me—
waiting for you to want me
and tell me: "Now."

Para vivir no quiero
islas, palacios, torres.
¡Qué alegría más alta:
vivir en los pronombres!

Quítate ya los trajes,
las señas, los retratos;
yo no te quiero así,
disfrazada de otra,
hija siempre de algo.
Te quiero pura, libre,
irreductible: tú.
Sé que cuando te llame
entre todas las gentes
del mundo,
sólo tú serás tú.
Y cuando me preguntes
quién es el que te llama,
el que te quiere suya,
enterraré los nombres,
los rótulos, la historia.
Iré rompiendo todo
lo que encima me echaron
desde antes de nacer.
Y vuelto ya al anónimo

To live my life I don't want
islands, palaces, towers.
What higher joy
to live in pronouns!

Leave your clothes,
identifications, photographs.
I don't want you like that,
disguised as someone else,
always somebody's daughter.
I want you pure, free,
irreducible: you.
I know that when I call you
from all the people
in the world—
only you will be you.
And when you ask me
who's calling you,
who's wanting you for his own,
I'll bury names,
labels, history.
I'll be breaking apart everything
heaped upon me
since before I was born.
And having returned to the eternal

eterno del desnudo,
de la piedra, del mundo,
te diré:
"Yo te quiero, soy yo."

anonymity of the naked,
of the stone, of the world,
I'll tell you:
"I love you, it's me."

Amor, amor, catástrofe.
¡Qué hundimiento del mundo!
Un gran horror a techos
quiebra columnas, tiempos;
los reemplaza por cielos
intemporales. Andas, ando
por entre escombros
de estíos y de inviernos
derrumbados. Se extinguen
las normas y los pesos.
Toda hacia atrás la vida
se va quitando siglos,
frenética, de encima;
desteje, galopando,
su curso, lento antes;
se desvive de ansia
de borrarse la historia,
de no ser más que el puro
anhelo de empezarse
otra vez. El futuro
se llama ayer. Ayer
oculto, secretísimo,
que se nos olvidó
y hay que reconquistar
con la sangre y el alma,
detrás de aquellos otros

Love, love, catastrophe.
What a collapse of the world!
A horrible blast on the roofs
smashes columns, centuries,
replaces them with timeless
skies. You go, I go
through rubble
of summers and shattered
winters. Weights
and standards become extinct.
All life goes backward,
frantically stripping itself
of centuries,
raveling, at a gallop,
its course that once was slow,
exhausting itself in the yearning
to obliterate history,
be only sheer
longing to begin
again. The future's
called yesterday: most hidden,
secret yesterday,
which we forgot,
and which we must recover
with blood and soul,
back of those other

ayeres conocidos.
¡Atrás y siempre atrás!
¡Retrocesos, en vértigo,
por dentro, hacia el mañana!
¡Que caiga todo! Ya
lo siento apenas. Vamos,
a fuerza de besar,
inventando las ruinas
del mundo, de la mano
tú y yo
por entre el gran fracaso
de la flor y del orden.
Y ya siento entre tactos,
entre abrazos, tu piel
que me entrega el retorno
al palpitar primero,
sin luz, antes del mundo,
total, sin forma, caos.

known yesterdays.
Back! Always back!
Backtracking, dizzily,
inward, toward tomorrow!
Let everything collapse! Now I hardly
feel it. Let's go on,
with the help of kisses,
inventing the ruins
of the world, hand in hand,
you and I,
in the midst of the total failure
of flower and order.
And now as I touch, as I embrace,
I feel your skin
giving me the way back
to the first pulsation
before light was, before the world was:
total, formless, chaos.

¡Sí, todo con exceso:
la luz, la vida, el mar!
Plural todo, plural,
luces, vidas y mares.
A subir, a ascender
de docenas a cientos,
de cientos a millar,
en una jubilosa
repetición sin fin,
de tu amor, unidad.
Tables, plumas y máquinas,
todo a multiplicar,
caricia por caricia,
abrazo por volcán.
Hay que cansar los números.
Que cuenten sin parar,
que se embriaguen contando,
y que no sepan ya
cuál de ellos será el último:
¡qué vivir sin final!
Que un gran tropel de ceros
asalte nuestras dichas
esbeltas, al pasar,
y las lleve a su cima.
Que se rompan la cifras,
sin poder cacular

Yes, everything in excess:
light, life, sea!
Plural, everything plural,
lights, lives, and seas.
To rise, to ascend
from dozens to hundreds,
from hundreds to a thousand,
in a joyous
endless repetition
of your love, of oneness.
Boards, feathers, and engines,
everything multiplying,
caress on caress,
by ardent embrace.
We must exhaust the numbers.
Let them count without stopping,
let them get dizzy counting,
and don't let them ever know
which of them will be the last!
O to live without an ending!
Let a great rush of zeros
assault our graceful
fortunes, in passing,
and carry them to the peak.
Let the ciphers burst
without managing to compute

ni el tiempo ni los besos.
Y al otro lado ya
de cómputos, de sinos,
entregarnos a ciegas
—¡exceso, qué penúltimo!—
a un gran fondo azaroso
que irresistiblemente
está
cantándonos a gritos
fúlgidos de futuro:
"Eso no es nada, aún.
Buscaos bien, hay más."

the time or the kisses.
And now beyond
computations, beyond destinies,
let us surrender blindly—
next-to-the-last excess!—
to a great perilous depth
irresistibly
singing to us
in a voice loud
and bright with the future:
"That's nothing, so far.
Search well within yourselves, there's more."

¡Qué entera cae la piedra!
Nada disiente en ella
de su destino, de su ley: el suelo.
No te expliques tu amor, ni me lo expliques;
obedecerlo basta. Cierra
los ojos, las preguntas, húndete
en tu querer, la ley anticipando
por voluntad, llenándolo de síes,
de banderas, de gozos,
ese otro hundirse que detrás aguarda,
de la muerte fatal. Mejor no amarse
mirándose en espejos complacidos,
deshaciendo
esa gran unidad en juegos vanos;
mejor no amarse
con alas, por el aire,
como las mariposas o las nubes,
flotantes. Busca pesos,
los más hondos, en ti, que ellos te arrastren
a ese gran centro donde yo te espero.
Amor total, quererse como masas.

How the stone falls as a whole!
Nothing in it dissents
from its destiny, from its law: the ground.
Don't explain your love to yourself, nor to me;
to obey is enough. Shut
your eyes, your questions, submerse yourself
in your loving—filling it with yeses,
with banners, with delights,
anticipating with your will the law,
that other submersion which waits behind it,
in inevitable death. Better not to love each other
looking at each other in pleasing mirrors,
destroying
that great unity in frivolous games;
better not to love each other
on wings, in the air,
like butterflies or clouds
floating. Search for weights, the deepest,
in yourself, let them drag you down
to that profound center where I wait for you.
Total love, as the love of mass for mass.

¡Ay, cuántas cosas perdidas
que no se perdieron nunca!
Todas las guardabas tú.

Menudos granos de tiempo,
que un día se llevó el aire.
Alfabetos de la espuma,
que un día se llevó el mar.
Yo por perdidos los daba.

Y por perdidas las nubes
que yo quise sujetar
en el cielo
clavándolas con miradas.
Y las alegrías altas
del querer, y las angustias
de estar aún queriendo poco,
y las ansias
de querer, quererte, más.
Todo por perdido, todo
en el haber sido antes,
en el no ser nunca, ya.

Y entonces viniste tú
de lo oscuro, iluminada
de joven paciencia honda,

54

O how many things lost
that never got lost!
You were keeping them all.

Tiny grains of time,
that the wind carried off one day.
Alphabets of foam
that the sea carried off one day.
I considered them lost.

And lost the clouds
that I tried to fasten
in the sky,
nailing them down with glances.
And the intense joys
of loving, and the pangs
of still loving too little,
and the longing
to love, to love you, more.
Everything lost, everything,
having taken place before,
never to be again.

And then you came
out of the dark, illumined
by deep young patience,

ligera, sin que pesara
sobre tu cintura fina,
sobre tus hombros desnudos,
el pasado que traías
tú, tan joven, para mí.
Cuando te miré a los besos
vírgenes que tú me diste,
los tiempos y las espumas,
las nubes y los amores
que perdí estaban salvados.
Si de mí se me escaparon,
no fue para ir a morirse
en la nada.
En ti seguían viviendo.
Lo que yo llamaba olvido
eras tú.

lightly, without the past weighing
on your slender waist,
your bare shoulders—
the past that you, so young,
were bringing to me.
When I gazed at you in the virginal
kisses you gave me,
seasons and surfs,
clouds and loves
that I'd lost were saved.
If they'd slipped away from me,
they weren't going to die
in nothingness.
They would continue living in you.
What I was calling forgotten,
was you.

Ahí, detrás de la risa,
ya no se te conoce.
Vas y vienes, resbalas
por un mundo de valses
helados, cuesta abajo;
y al pasar, los caprichos,
los prontos te arrebatan
besos sin vocación,
a ti, la momentánea
cautiva de lo fácil.
"¡Qué alegre!", dicen todos.
Y es que entonces estás
queriendo ser tú otra,
pareciéndote tanto
a ti misma, que tengo
miedo a perderte, así.

Te sigo. Espero. Sé
que cuando no te miren
túneles ni luceros,
cuando se crea el mundo
que ya sabe quién eres
y diga: "Sí, ya sé",
tú te desatarás,
con los brazos en alto,
por detrás de tu pelo,

Back there, behind your laughter,
no one really knows you.
You come and go, you glide
through a world of icy
waltzes, downward;
and as you pass, whims,
sudden impulses snatch
casual kisses
from you, the momentary
captive of what's easy.
"How light-hearted!" they all say.
And that's just when you're
trying to be the other you,
resembling yourself
so closely, I'm afraid
of losing you, that way.

I follow you. I wait. I know
that when tunnels and stars
aren't watching you,
when the world believes
it really knows who you are
and says, "Yes, I know very well,"
you'll loosen the knot,
with your hands lifted
behind your head

la lazada, mirándome.
Sin ruido de cristal
se caerá por el suelo,
ingrávida careta
inútil ya, la risa.
Y al verte en el amor
que yo te tiendo siempre
como un espejo ardiendo,
tú reconocerás
un rostro serio, grave,
una desconocida
alta, pálida y triste,
que es mi amada. Y me quiere
por detrás de la risa.

while you gaze at me.
With no shattering of glass,
your laugh will fall
to the ground: weightless mask
no longer of use.
And seeing yourself in the love
I reach out to you always
like a burning mirror,
you'll recognize
a serious grave countenance,
an unknown person,
exalted, pale, and sad,
who is my beloved. And she loves me,
back of her laughter.

¿Por qué pregunto dónde estás
si no estoy ciego,
si tú no estás ausente?
Si te veo,
ir y venir,
a ti, a tu cuerpo alto
que se termina en voz,
como en humo la llama,
en el aire, impalpable.

Y te pregunto, sí,
y te pregunto de qué eres,
de quién;
y abres los brazos
y me enseñas
la alta imagen de ti,
y me dices que mía.

Y te pregunto, siempre.

Why am I asking where you are
if I'm not blind,
if you're not absent?
If I see you,
coming and going,
you, your tall body
that ends in your voice,
as the flame in smoke,
in the air, impalpable.

And I'm asking you, yes,
and I ask you what you are,
and whose;
and you open your arms
and show me
the tall figure of yourself,
and you tell me it's mine.

And I keep asking you.

Yo no puedo darte más.
No soy más que lo que soy.

¡Ay, cómo quisiera ser
arena, sol, en estío!
Que te tendieses
descansada a descansar.
Que me dejaras
tu cuerpo al marcharte, huella
tierna, tibia, inolvidable.
Y que contigo se fuese
sobre ti, mi beso lento:
color,
desde la nuca al talón,
moreno.

¡Ay, cómo quisiera ser
vidrio, o estofa o madera
que conserva su color
aquí, su perfume aquí,
y nació a tres mil kilómetros!
Ser
la materia que te gusta,
que tocas todos los días
y que ves ya sin mirar
a tu alrededor, las cosas

I can't give you more.
I'm no more than what I am.

O how I wish I were
sand, sun, in summertime!
That you were stretched out
to rest, resting.
That you'd leave me
your body when you go away: delicate
trace, warm, unforgettable.
And that my lingering kiss
might go with you:
your color,
from nape to heel,
sun-brown.

O how I wish I were
glass or cloth or wood
that keeps its color
here, its fragrance here,
though born three thousand kilometers away!
Wish I were
the thing you like,
that you touch every day
and see without even looking
around you, the things—

—collar, frasco, seda antigua—
que cuando tú echas de menos
preguntas: "¡Ay!, ¿dónde está?"

¡Y, ay, cómo quisiera ser
una alegría entre todas,
una sola, la alegría
con que te alegraras tú!
Un amor, un amor solo:
el amor del que tú te enamorases.

Pero
no soy más que lo que soy.

necklace, bottle, antique silk—
about which, when you miss them,
you ask, "O where is it?"

And o how I wish I were
one joy among them all,
a single one, the joy
in which you'd rejoice!
A love, a single love:
the love you'd fall in love with.

But
I'm no more than what I am.

¿Regalo, don, entrega?
Símbolo puro, signo
de que me quiero dar.
Qué dolor, separarme
de aquello que te entrego
y que te pertenece
sin más destino ya
que ser tuyo, de ti,
mientras que yo me quedo
en la otra orilla, solo,
todavía tan mío.
Cómo quisiera ser
eso que yo te doy
y no quien te lo da.
Cuando te digo:
"Soy tuyo, sólo tuyo",
tengo miedo a una nube,
a una ciudad, a un número
que me pueden robar
un minuto al amor
entero a ti debido.
¡Ah!, si fuera la rosa
que te doy; la que estuvo
en riesgo de ser otra
y no para tus manos,
mientras no llegué yo.

Gift, bestowal, surrender?
Pure symbol, sign
that I want to give myself.
How painful, to separate myself
from what I surrender to you,
what belongs to you
with no further destination now
beyond being yours, belonging to you,
while I remain
on the other shore, alone,
still belonging so much to myself.
How I'd like to be
what I give you
and not the one who gives it to you.
When I say to you:
"I'm yours, only yours,"
I'm afraid of a cloud,
a city, a number
that may steal
a minute from the total
love owed to you.
O! if I were the rose
I give you, the one
that risked being another
and not for your hands,
until I arrived.

La que no tendrá ahora
más futuro que ser
con tu rosa, mi rosa,
vivida en ti, por ti,
en su olor, en su tacto.
Hasta que tú la asciendas
sobre su deshojarse
a un recuerdo de rosa,
segura, inmarcesible,
puesta ya toda a salvo
de otro amor u otra vida
que los que vivas tú.

The one that now will have
no other future except to be
at once your rose and my rose,
lived in you, through you,
in its fragrance, in its touch!
Until you lift it
above its shedding of leaves
to a remembrance of rose,
sure, unfading,
now made entirely safe
from any love or any life other
than what you are living.

El sueño es una larga
despedida de ti.
¡Qué gran vida contigo,
en pie, alerta en el sueño!
¡Dormir el mundo, el sol,
las hormigas, las horas,
todo, todo dormido,
en el sueño que duermo!
Menos tú, tú la única,
viva, sobrevivida,
en el sueño que sueño.

Pero sí, despedida:
voy a dejarte. Cerca,
la mañana prepara
toda su precisión
de rayos y de risas.
¡Afuera, afuera, ya,
lo soñado, flotante,
marchando sobre el mundo,
sin poderlo pisar
porque no tiene sitio,
desesperadamente!

Te abrazo por vez última:
eso es abrir los ojos.

Sleep is a prolonged
leave-taking from you.
What a splendid life with you,
up and alert in sleep!
The world sleeping, the sun,
the ants, the hours,
everything, everything asleep
in the sleep I'm sleeping!
Except you, the only one,
lively, living on,
in the dream I'm dreaming.

But still, a leave-taking:
I'm going to leave you. Close at hand,
the morning's preparing
all its exact
rays and laughs.
Time, now, to get rid
of what's dreamed, floating,
moving over the world,
desperately,
unable to step down,
not having any place.

I embrace you for the last time:
that's when I open my eyes.

Ya está. Las verticales
entran a trabajar,
sin un desmayo, en reglas.
Los colores ejercen
sus oficios de azul,
de rosa, verde, todos
a la hora en punto. El mundo
va a funcionar hoy bien:
me ha matado ya el sueño.
Te siento huir, ligera,
de la aurora, exactísima,
hacia arriba, buscando
la que no se ve estrella,
el desorden celeste,
que es sólo donde cabes.
Luego, cuando despierto,
no te conozco, casi,
cuando, a mi lado, tiendes
los brazos hacia mí
diciendo: "¿Qué soñaste?"
Y te contestaría:
"No sé, se me ha olvidado",
si no estuviera ya
tu cuerpo limpio, exacto,
ofreciéndome en labios
el gran error del día.

It's done. Verticals
start to work
without faltering, according to rule.
Colors perform
their function of blue,
red, green, all
precisely on the hour. The world
is going to function well today:
it's already killed my dream.
I feel you escaping, swiftly,
from dawn, most punctually,
upward, seeking
the invisible star,
celestial disorder,
which alone holds you.
Then, as I wake,
I scarcely know you
when, at my side, you reach
your arms toward me,
saying, "What did you dream?"
And I'd answer:
"I don't know, I've forgotten"—
if your fresh, precise body
weren't already
offering me on the lips
the day's supreme error.

Cuando cierras los ojos
tus párpados son aire.
Me arrebatan:
me voy contigo, adentro.

No se ve nada, no
se oye nada. Me sobran
los ojos y los labios,
en este mundo tuyo.
Para sentirte a ti
no sirven
los sentidos de siempre,
usados con los otros.
Hay que esperar los nuevos.
Se anda a tu lado
sordamente, en lo oscuro,
tropezando en acasos,
en vísperas; hundiéndose
hacia arriba
con un gran peso de alas.

Cuando vuelves a abrir
los ojos yo me vuelvo
afuera, ciego ya,
tropezando también,
sin ver, tampoco, aquí.

When you close your eyes
your eyelids are a breath of wind.
They carry me off:
I go with you, inside.

Nothing's to be seen, nothing
to be heard. I don't need
eyes and lips,
in this world of yours.
In perceiving you,
the ordinary senses,
used for others,
won't help.
I have to wait for new ones.
I walk by your side
dumbly, in the dark,
stumbling on chances,
anticipations; plunging
upward
with a huge weight of wings.

When you open your eyes
again I return
to the outside, blind now,
stumbling too,
unable to see here, either.

77

Sin saber más vivir
ni en el otro, en el tuyo,
ni en este
mundo descolorido
en donde yo vivía.
Inútil, desvalido
entre los dos.
Yendo, viniendo
de uno a otro
cuando tú quieres,
cuando abres, cuando cierras
los párpados, los ojos.

No longer knowing how to live
either in the other world, yours,
or in this
faded world
where I was living.
Useless, disabled
between the two.
Going, coming
from the one to the other
when you want me to,
when you open, when you close
your eyelids, your eyes.

PART II

Ya está la ventana abierta.
Tenía que ser así
el día.
Azul el cielo, sí, azul
indudable, como anoche
le iban queriendo tus besos.
Henchida la luz de viento
y tensa igual que una vela
que lleva el día, velero,
por los mundos a su fin:
porque anoche tú quisiste
que tú y yo nos embarcáramos
en un alba que llegaba.
Tenía que ser así.
Y todo,
las aves de por el aire,
las olas de por el mar,
gozosamente animado:
con el ánima
misma que estaba latiendo
en las olas y los vuelos
nocturnos del abrazar.
Si los cielos iluminan
trasluces de paraíso,
islas de color de edén,
es que en las horas sin luz,

Now the window's been opened.
The day had to be
like this.
The sky blue, yes, absolutely
blue, the way your kisses
last night wanted it.
The light's filled with wind,
and stretched as a sail
that bears the swift-sailing day
through the spheres to its ending:
because last night you wanted us
to embark, you and me,
on an oncoming dawn.
It had to be this way.
And everything,
birds through the air,
waves in the sea,
joyously alive:
with the same
spirit that was throbbing
in the waves and the night flights
of our embrace.
If the skies light up
glimmerings of paradise,
islands the color of Eden,
that's because in the hours without light,

sin suelo, hemos anhelado
la tierra más inocente
y jardín para los dos.
Y el mundo es hoy como es hoy
porque lo querías tú,
porque anoche lo quisimos.

Un día
es el gran rastro de luz
que deja el amor detrás
cuando cruza por la noche,
sin él eterna, del mundo.
Es lo que quieren dos seres
si se quieren hacia un alba.
Porque un día nunca sale
de almanaques ni horizontes:
es la hechura sonrosada,
la forma viva del ansia
de dos almas en amor,
que entre abrazos, a lo largo
de la noche, beso a beso,
se buscan su claridad.
Al encontrarla amanece,
ya no es suya, ya es del mundo.
Y sin saber lo que hicieron,
los amantes
echan a andar por su obra,
que parece un día más.

without ground, we have longed
for earth more innocent
and a garden for us two.
And the world's as it is today
because you wanted it,
because last night we wanted it.

A day
is the great trail of light
that love leaves behind
as it passes through the world's night—
unending, otherwise.
It's what two beings desire
if they love toward a dawn.
Because a day never arises
out of almanacs or horizons:
it's the rose-colored creation,
the living form of the yearning
of two souls in love,
who among embraces, the length
of night, kiss on kiss,
are seeking their own clear light.
When they find it, day breaks,
no longer theirs, but the world's now.
And without knowing what they did,
the lovers
begin moving through their work,
which has the look of one day more.

Me quedaría en todo
lo que estoy, donde estoy.
Quieto en el agua quieta;
de plomo, hundido, sordo
en el amor sin sol.
¡Qué ansia de repetirse
en esto que está siendo!
¡Qué afán de que mañana
sea
nada más que llenar
otra vez al tenderte
ese hueco que deja
hoy exacto en la arena
tu cuerpo!
Ni futuro, ni nuevo
el horizonte. Esto
apretado y estrecho:
tela, carne y el mar.
Nada promete el mundo:
lo da, lo tengo ya.
Nunca me iré de ti
por el viento, en las velas,
por el alma, cantando,
ni por los trenes, no.
Si me marcho será
que estoy
viviendo contra mí.

I'd like to stay exactly
the way I am, where I am.
In still water, be still:
leaden, sunken, soundless
in a love without sun.
What longing to repeat one's self
in this business of being!
What craving that tomorrow
you simply
stretch out
filling precisely that hollow
which today
your body leaves
in the sand.
No future, no new
horizon. Just this
held tight:
cloth, flesh, and sea.
The world promises nothing:
it gives, and I already have that.
I'll never leave you,
not on the wind filling the sail,
nor on the song of my soul,
nor by train, never.
If I go, it will be
that I'm living
contrary to myself.

¿Tú sabes lo que eres
de mí?
¿Sabes tú el nombre?

                    No es
el que todos te llaman,
esa palabra usada
que se dicen las gentes,
si besan o se quieren,
porque ya se lo han dicho
otros que se besaron.
Yo no lo sé, lo digo,
se me asoma a los labios
como una aurora virgen
de la que no soy dueño.
Tú tampoco lo sabes,
lo oyes. Y lo recibe
tu oído igual que el silencio
que nos llega hasta el alma
sin saber de qué ausencias
de ruidos está hecho.
¿Son letras, son sonidos?
Es mucho más antiguo.
Lengua de paraíso,
sones primeros, vírgenes
tanteos de los labios,

Do you know what you are
to me?
Do you know the name?

           It isn't
what they all call you,
that worn-out word
people say to each other
if they kiss or love,
because it's been said already
by others who kissed.
I don't know the name, I say it,
it appears on my lips
like a fresh dawn
over which I have no control.
You don't know it either,
you hear it. And your ear
receives it just like silence
which reaches the soul
without our knowing what absence
of noises it's made of.
Are they letters, are they sounds?
It's much more ancient.
Language of paradise,
primordial sounds, virginal
attempts of lips,

cuando, antes de los números,
en el aire del mundo
se estrenaban los nombres
de los gozos primeros. .
Que se olvidaban luego
para llamarlo todo
de otro modo al hacerlo
otra vez: nuevo son
para el júbilo nuevo.
En ese paraíso
de los tiempos del alma,
allí, en el más antiguo,
es donde está tu nombre.
Y aunque yo te lo llamo
en mi vida, a tu vida,
con mi boca, a tu oído,
en esta realidad,
como él no deja huella
en memoria ni en signo,
y apenas lo percibes,
nítido y momentáneo,
a su cielo se vuelve
todo alado de olvido,
dicho parece en sueños,
sólo en sueños oído.
Y así, lo que tú eres,
cuando yo te lo digo
no podrá serlo nadie,
nadie podrá decírtelo.
Porque ni tú ni yo
conocemos su nombre
que sobre mí desciende,
pasajero de labios,

when, before numbers,
in the air of the world
they were trying out the names
of their first delights.
Which they would then forget
in order to call everything
something else as they tried it
again: new sound
for the new joy.
In that paradise
of the times of the soul,
in furthest antiquity,
that's where your name is.
And though I call you this,
in my life, to your life,
with my mouth, to your ear,
in this real world:
since it leaves no trace
in memory or in a sign,
and you barely perceive it,
bright and fleeting—
it returns to its heaven
all winged with forgetfulness,
it seems to have been said in dreams,
heard only in dreams.
And thus, what you are,
when I say it to you,
no one can be,
no one can say it to you.
Because neither you nor I
know its name—
descending upon me,
passing over the lips,

huésped
fugaz de los oídos
cuando desde mi alma
lo sientes en la tuya,
sin poderlo aprender,
sin saberlo yo mismo.

momentary
visitor in the ears—
as it issues from my soul
and is felt by you in yours,
though you can't grasp it,
though I myself don't know it.

¡Cuánto tiempo fuiste dos!
Querías y no querías.
No eras como tu querer,
ni tu querer como tú.
¡Qué vaivén entre una y otra!
A los espejos del mundo,
al silencio, a los azares,
preguntabas
cuál sería la mejor.
Inconstante de ti misma
siempre te estabas matando
tu mismo sí con tu no.
Y en el borde de los besos,
ni tu corazón ni el mío,
sabía quien se acercaba:
si era la que tú querías
o la que quería yo.
Cuando estábais separadas,
como la flor de su flor,
¡qué lejos de ti tenía
que ir a buscarte el querer!
Él estaba por un lado.
Tú en otro.
Lo encontraba. Pero no
sabía estarme con él,
vivir así separados

How long there were two of you!
You loved and you didn't love.
You didn't resemble your love,
nor did your love resemble you.
What coming and going between the one and the other!
You kept asking
the mirrors of this world,
silence, chance,
which would be the better one.
Unfaithful to yourself
you always kept killing
your own yes with your no.
And on the verge of your kisses,
neither your heart nor mine
knew who was drawing close:
whether it was the one you wanted
or the one I wanted.
When you were separated,
as the flower from the flower,
how far from you I had to go
in search of your love!
It remained on one side.
You on the other.
I kept finding it. But
I didn't know how to stay with it,
to live in separation that way,

o de tu amor o de ti.
Yo os quería a los dos.
Y por fin junto está todo.
Cara a cara te miraste,
tu mirada en ti te vio:
eras ya la que querías.
Y ahora os beso a las dos
en ti sola.
Y esta paz de ser entero,
no sabe
el alma quién la ganó:
si es que tu amor se parece
a ti, de tanto quererte,
o es que tú,
de tanto estarle queriendo,
eres ya igual que tu amor.

either from your love or from you.
I loved you both.
And at last everything's come together.
You looked at yourself face to face,
your glance saw you in yourself:
you were now the one that was in love.
And now I kiss you both
in you alone.
And the soul doesn't know
who won
this serenity of being whole:
whether your love resembles
you, from wanting you so,
or you,
from wanting it so,
are now the same as your love.

Lo que eres
me distrae de lo que dices.

Lanzas palabras veloces,
empavesadas de risas,
invitándome
a ir adonde ellas me lleven.
No te atiendo, no las sigo:
estoy mirando
los labios donde nacieron.

Miras de pronto a lo lejos.
Clavas la mirada allí,
no sé en qué, y se te dispara
a buscarlo ya tu alma
afilada, de saeta.
Yo no miro adonde miras:
yo te estoy viendo mirar.

Y cuando deseas algo
no pienso en lo que tú quieres,
ni lo envidio: es lo de menos.
Lo quieres hoy, lo deseas;
mañana lo olvidarás
por una querencia nueva.
No. Te espero más allá

98

What you are
distracts me from what you say.

You hurl swift words
bedecked with laughs,
inviting me
to go where they may take me.
I don't listen to you, I don't follow them:
I'm looking
at the lips they sprung from.

Suddenly you look into the distance.
You fasten your gaze there,
I don't know on what, and away
goes your soul in search of it—
sharpened, like an arrow.
I don't know where you're looking:
I'm seeing you looking.

And when you desire something,
I don't think about what you want,
nor envy it: that's the least of it.
You want it today, you desire it;
tomorrow you'll forget it
for a new hankering.
No, I wait for you beyond

de los fines y los términos.
En lo que no ha de pasar
me quedo, en el puro acto
de tu deseo, queriéndote.
Y no quiero ya otra cosa
más que verte a ti querer.

endings and boundaries.
What won't come to an end,
the pure act of your desire,
that's what I'll stay with, loving you.
And I want nothing more
than to watch you desiring.

La forma de querer tú
es dejarme que te quiera.
El sí con que te me rindes
es el silencio. Tus besos
son ofrecerme los labios
para que los bese yo.
Jamás palabras, abrazos,
me dirán que tú existías,
que me quisiste: jamás.
Me lo dicen hojas blancas,
mapas, augurios, teléfonos;
tú, no.
Y estoy abrazado a ti
sin preguntarte, de miedo
a que no sea verdad
que tú vives y me quieres.
Y estoy abrazado a ti
sin mirar y sin tocarte.
No vaya a ser que descubra
con preguntas, con caricias,
esa soledad inmensa
de quererte sólo yo.

Your way of loving
is to let me love you.
The yes with which you yield to me
is silence. You kiss
by offering your lips
for me to kiss.
Never will words, embraces
tell me that you existed,
that you loved me: never.
Blank pages tell me,
maps, auguries, telephones;
not you.
And I'm clasped to you
without asking you, for fear
it's not true
that you're alive and you love me.
And I'm clasped to you
without looking at you and touching you.
Lest I discover
with questions, and caresses,
that immense solitude
of being the only one in love.

¡Qué probable eres tú!
Si los ojos me dicen,
mirándote, que no,
que no eres de verdad,
las manos y los labios,
con los ojos cerrados,
recorren tiernas pruebas:
la lenta convicción
de tu ser, va ascendiendo
por escala de tactos,
de bocas, carne y carne.
Si tampoco lo creo,
algo más denso ya,
más palpable, la voz
con que dices: "Te quiero",
lucha para afirmarte
contra mi duda. Al lado
un cuerpo besa, abraza,
frenético, buscándose
su realidad aquí
en mí que no la creo;
besa
para lograr su vida
todavía indecisa,
puro milagro, en mí.
Y lentamente vas

How probable you are!
If my eyes gazing at you
tell me, no,
you don't really exist,
my hands and lips,
with my eyes closed,
discover delicate proofs:
the gradual conviction
of your existence goes climbing up
the ladder of touch,
of mouths, flesh to flesh.
If I don't believe that either,
something still more substantial,
more palpable, the voice
with which you say, "I love you,"
struggles to affirm you
against my doubt. Beside me
a body's kissing, embracing,
frantically seeking
its reality here
in me, who don't believe in it;
kissing
in order to achieve its life,
still uncertain,
sheer miracle, in me.
And gradually,

formándote tú misma,
naciéndote,
dentro de tu querer,
de mi querer, confusos,
como se forma el día
en la gran duda oscura.
Y agoniza la antigua
criatura dudosa
que tú dejas atrás,
inútil ser de antes,
para que surja al fin
la irrefutable tú,
desnuda Venus cierta,
entre auroras seguras,
que se gana a sí misma
su nuevo ser, queriéndome.

you are forming yourself,
giving birth to yourself,
within your love,
my love, mingled,
as day forms itself
within the great dark doubt.
And the old doubtful
creature you leave
behind, lies in death's agony—
a useless being from before—
so that there arises in the end
the undeniable you,
naked Venus, confident
among certain dawns
that she's achieving for herself
her new being, by loving me.

Perdóname por ir así buscándote
tan torpemente, dentro
de ti.
Perdóname el dolar, alguna vez.
Es que quiero sacar
de ti tu mejor tú.
Ese que no te viste y que yo veo,
nadador por tu fondo, preciosísimo.
Y cogerlo
y tenerlo yo en alto como tiene
el árbol la luz última
que le ha encontrado al sol.
Y entonces tú
en su busca vendrías, a lo alto.
Para llegar a él
subida sobre ti, como te quiero,
tocando ya tan sólo a tu pasado
con las puntas rosadas de tus pies,
en tensión todo el cuerpo, ya ascendiendo
de ti a ti misma.

Y que a mi amor entonces, le conteste
la nueva criatura que tú eras.

Forgive my searching for you
so clumsily,
inside you.
Forgive my hurting you at times.
I want to extract
from you your better you.
The one that you didn't see in yourself and that I see:
swimmer in your most precious depths.
And to catch it
and hold it up high,
as a tree holds the last light
it has found in the sun.
And then you'd come
in search of it, high overhead.
To reach it,
you'd be lifted above yourself, the way I love you,
touching your past
only with the rosy tips of your toes,
your body straining, rising now
from you to yourself.

And let my love be answered
by the newborn person you were.

¡Qué paseo de noche
con tu ausencia a mi lado!
Me acompaña el sentir
que no vienes conmigo.
Los espejos, el agua
se creen que voy solo;
se lo creen los ojos.
Sirenas de los cielos
aún chorreando estrellas,
tiernas muchachas lánguidas,
que salen de automóviles,
me llaman. No las oigo.
Aún tengo en el oído
tu voz, cuando me dijo:
"No te vayas." Y ellas,
tus tres palabras últimas,
van hablando conmigo
sin cesar, me contestan
a lo que preguntó
mi vida el primer día.
Espectros, sombras, sueños,
amores de otra vez,
de mí compadecidos,
quieren venir conmigo,
van a darme la mano.
Pero notan de pronto

What a walk in the night
with your absence at my side!
I'm kept company by the feeling
that you're not coming with me.
Mirrors, water
think I'm walking alone;
their eyes think so.
Sirens of the skies
still dripping stars,
delicate languid girls,
stepping out of automobiles,
call to me. I don't hear them.
In my ears I still keep
your voice, as it said to me:
"Don't go away." And those
last three words of yours
go on speaking to me
incessantly, they answer
the question my life asked
on the first day.
Phantoms, shadows, dreams,
loves of former times,
out of compassion for me,
want to come with me,
start to give me their hand.
But they notice suddenly

que yo llevo estrechada,
cálida, viva, tierna,
la forma de una mano
palpitando en la mía.
La que tú me tendiste
al decir: "No te vayas."
Se van, se marchan ellos,
los espectros, las sombras,
atónitos de ver
que no me dejan solo.
Y entonces la alta noche,
la oscuridad, el frío,
engañados también,
me vienen a besar.
No pueden; otro beso
se interpone, en mis labios.
No se marcha de allí,
no se irá. El que me diste,
mirándome a los ojos
cuando yo me marché,
diciendo: "No te vayas."

that I'm holding tight
the shape of a hand,
warm, vibrant, soft,
throbbing in mine.
The hand you held out to me,
saying, "Don't go away."
They're going, they're moving away,
the phantoms, the shadows,
astonished to see
they're not leaving me alone.
And then deep night,
darkness, cold,
also mistaken,
approach to kiss me.
They can't; another kiss
intercedes on my lips.
It doesn't leave,
it won't go away. The kiss you gave me
when I left,
as you gazed into my eyes
saying, "Don't go away."

Imposible llamarla.
Yo no dormía. Ella
creyó que yo dormía.
Y la dejé hacer todo:
ir quitándome
poco a poco la luz
sobre los ojos.
Dominarse los pasos,
el respirar, cambiada
en querencia de sombra
que no estorbara nunca
con el bulto o el ruido.
Y marcharse despacio,
despacio, con el alma,
para dejar detrás
de la puerta, al salir,
un ser que descansara.
Para no despertarme,
a mí, que no dormía.
Y no pude llamarla.
Sentir que me quería,
quererme, entonces, era
irse con los demás,
hablar fuerte, reír,
pero lejos, segura
de que yo no la oiría.

Impossible to call out to her.
I wasn't sleeping. She
thought I was sleeping.
And I let her do everything:
go around shutting out
little by little
the light from my eyes.
And control her footsteps,
her breathing, changed
into a shadow's desire
never to disturb
with bulk or noise.
And slip away slowly,
slowly, with her soul,
to leave behind the door,
as she went,
someone who would rest.
In order not to wake me—
and I wasn't asleep.
And I couldn't call out to her.
To feel she loved me,
to love me, then,
was to go off with the others,
talk loud, laugh,
but far away, certain
that I wouldn't hear her.

Liberada ya, alegre,
cogiendo mariposas
de espuma, sombras verdes
de olivos, toda llena
de gozo de saberme
en los brazos aquellos
a quienes me entregó
—sin celos, para siempre,
de su ausencia—, del sueño
mío, que no dormía.
Imposible llamarla.
Su gran obra de amor
era dejarme solo.

At liberty now, happy,
gathering butterflies
of foam, green shadows
of olive trees, filled
with the joy of knowing
I lay in those arms
into which she'd delivered me—
without jealousy, ever,
of her absence—those arms of that sleep
of mine, which I wasn't sleeping.
Impossible to call out to her.
Her great labor of love
was to let me stay alone.

Se te está viendo la otra.
Se parece a ti:
los pasos, el mismo ceño,
los mismos tacones altos
todos manchados de estrellas.
Cuando vayáis por la calle
juntas, las dos,
¡qué difícil el saber
quién eres, quién no eres tú!
Tan iguales ya, que sea
imposible vivir más
así, siendo tan iguales.
Y como tú eres la frágil,
la apenas siendo, tiernísima,
tú tienes que ser la muerta.
Tú dejarás que te mate,
que siga viviendo ella,
embustera, falsa tú,
pero tan igual a ti
que nadie se acordará
sino yo de lo que eras.
Y vendrá un día
—porque vendrá, sí, vendrá—
en que al mirarme a los ojos
tú veas
que pienso en ella y la quiero:
tú veas que no eres tú.

The other you is showing.
She resembles you:
footsteps, the same frown,
the same high heels
dotted all over with stars.
When you go along the street
together, the two of you,
how difficult to know
which you are, which you are not!
So alike now, maybe
you can't go on living
like this, being so alike.
And since you are the fragile one,
the scarcely existing, more delicate one,
you're the one that has to die.
You'll let her destroy you,
let her continue living,
imposter, the false you,
but so like you—
no one except myself
will remember what you were.
And a day will come—
because it will come, yes it will—
when looking into my eyes
you'll see
I'm thinking of her and loving her:
you'll see it's not you.

Entre tu verdad más honda
y yo
me pones siempre tus besos.
La presiento, cerca ya,
la deseo, no la alcanzo;
cuando estoy más cerca de ella
me cierras el paso tú,
te me ofreces en los labios.
Y ya no voy más allá.
Triunfas. Olvido, besando,
tu secreto encastillado.
Y me truecas el afán
de seguir más hacia ti,
en deseo
de que no me dejes ir
y me beses.
　　　　　Ten cuidado.
Te vas a vender, así.
Porque un día el beso tuyo,
de tan lejos, de tan hondo
te va a nacer,
que lo que estás escondiendo
detrás de él
te salte todo a los labios.
Y lo que tú me negabas

Between your deepest truth
and me
you always put your kisses.
I almost feel it, quite close,
I desire it, I don't reach it;
when I'm closest to it
you close off the way,
you offer me yourself on the lips.
And I get no further.
You win. I forget, in kissing,
your safely guarded secret.
And you turn my longing
to go on further toward you,
into wanting
you not to let me go,
and to kiss me.
                    Take care.
You're going to betray yourself, that way.
Because one day your kiss
is going to rise
from so far, from so deep,
that what you're hiding
behind it
will all spring to your lips.
And what you were denying me—

—alma delgada y esquiva—
se me entregue, me lo des
sin querer
donde querías negármelo.

tenuous and elusive soul—
will surrender itself to me, you'll give it to me
without wanting to,
where you wanted to deny it to me.

Mundo de lo prometido,
agua.
Todo es posible en el agua.

Apoyado en la baranda,
el mundo que está detrás
en el agua se me aclara,
y lo busco
en el agua, con los ojos,
con el alma, por el agua.
La montaña, cuerpo en rosa
desnuda, dura de siglos,
se me enternece en lo verde
líquido, rompe cadenas,
se escapa
dejando atrás su esqueleto,
ella fluyente, en el agua.
Los troncos rectos del árbol
entregan
su rectitud, ya cansada,
a las curvas tentaciones
de su reflejo en las ondas.
Y a las ramas, en enero,
—rebrillos de sol y espuma—,
les nacen hojas de agua.
Porque en el alma del río

World of what's promised:
water.
Everything is possible in water.

As I lean on the railing,
the world that lies behind
in the water becomes clear to me,
and I search for it
in the water, with my eyes,
with my soul, through the water.
The mountain, naked rose-red
body, hardened over centuries,
is softened for me in the green
liquid, it breaks chains,
escapes,
leaving its skeleton behind
as it flows in the water.
The straight tree trunks
surrender
their straightness, weary now,
to the curved beckoning
of their reflections in the waves.
And the branches, in January
resplendent with sun and foam—
grow leaves of water.
Because in the soul of the river

no hay inviernos:
de su fondo le florecen
cada mañana, a la orilla
tiernas primaveras blandas.
Los vastos fondos del tiempo,
de las distancias, se alisan
y se olvidan de su drama:
separar.
Todo se junta y se aplana.
El cielo más alto vive
confundido con la yerba,
como en el amor de Dios.
Y el que tiene amor remoto
mira en el agua, a su alcance,
imagen, voz, fabulosas
presencias de lo que ama.
Las órdenes terrenales
su filo embotan en ondas,
se olvidan de que nos mandan;
podemos, libres, querer
lo querido, por el agua.
Oscilan los imposibles,
tan trémulos como cañas
en la orilla, y a la rosa
y a la vida se le pierden
espinas que se clavaban.
De recta que va, de alegre,
el agua hacia su destino,
el terror de lo futuro
en su ejemplo se desarma:
si ella llega, llegaremos,
ella, nosotros, los dos,
al gran término del ansia.

there are no winters:
from its depth to the shore
tender mild springtimes
come into bloom every day.
The vast depths of time,
of distances, become smoothed out
and forget their drama:
separation.
Everything joins together and levels out.
The highest sky lives
mingled with grass,
as in God's love.
And the person who has a love far away
gazes into the water, within his reach,
fastening on image, voice, fabulous
presences of what he loves.
The orders of earth
dull their edge on waves,
they forget that they command us;
freed, we can love
what we've loved, in the water.
Impossible things tremble,
quivering like reeds
on the shore, and the rose
and life itself lose
their piercing thorns.
Water goes so directly,
so joyfully toward its destiny,
the terror of the future
is disarmed by its example:
if it arrives, we shall arrive,
both water and ourselves,
at the extreme limit of anguish.

Lo difícil en la tierra,
por la tierra,
triunfa gozoso en el agua.
Y mientras se están negando
—no constante, terrenal—
besos, auroras, mañanas,
aquí sobre el suelo firme,
el río seguro canta
los imposibles posibles,
de onda en onda, las promesas
de las dichas desatadas.

Todo lo niega la tierra,
pero todo se me da
en el agua, por el agua.

What's difficult on earth,
because of earth,
triumphs joyously in water.
And while kisses, dawns, mornings
are being refused—
the constant no of earth—
here on firm ground,
the confident river sings
impossible things becoming possible,
from wave to wave, promising
joys unbound.

Earth refuses everything:
but everything gives itself to me
in the water, through the water.

Dame tu libertad.
No quiero tu fatiga,
no, ni tus hojas secas,
tu sueño, ojos cerrados.
Ven a mí desde ti,
no desde tu cansancio
de ti. Quiero sentirla.
Tu libertad me trae,
igual que un viento universal,
un olor de maderas
remotas de tus muebles,
una bandada de visiones
que tú veías
cuando en el colmo de tu libertad
cerrabas ya los ojos.
¡Qué hermosa tú libre y en pie!
Si tú me das tu libertad me das tus años
blancos, limpios y agudos como dientes,
me das el tiempo en que tú la gozabas.
Quiero sentirla como siente el agua
del puerto, pensativa,
en las quillas inmóviles
el alta mar, la turbulencia sacra.
Sentirla,
vuelo parado,
igual que en sosegado soto

Give me your freedom.
I don't want your fatigue,
no, nor your dry leaves,
your dream, eyes closed.
Come to me from yourself,
not from your self-weariness.
I want to feel your freedom.
Like a universal wind,
it brings me
a fragrance of the exotic wood
your furniture's made of,
a flock of visions
you used to see
when, at the height of your freedom,
you'd finally close your eyes.
How handsome you are, free and erect!
If you give me your freedom, you give me
those years of yours, white, clear, sharp as teeth,
you give me the time when you were enjoying it.
I want to feel it as water,
pensive in the harbor,
feels heavy seas, holy turbulence,
against the motionless keels.
To feel it,
a halted wing,
as the bough

siente la rama
donde el ave se posa,
el ardor de volar, la lucha terca
contra las dimensiones en azul.
Descánsala hoy en mí: la gozaré
con un temblor de hoja en que se paran
gotas del cielo al suelo.
La quiero
para soltarla, solamente.
No tengo cárcel para ti en mi ser.
Tu libertad te guarda para mí.
La soltaré otra vez, y por el cielo,
por el mar, por el tiempo,
veré cómo se marcha hacia su sino.
Si su sino soy yo, te está esperando.

in the quiet grove feels—
when the bird alights—
the heat of flight, the hard struggle
against the expanse of blue.
Let it rest in me today: I'll enjoy it
as the tremor of a leaf upon which raindrops
touch on their way from the sky to the ground.
I want it
only to set it free.
I have no prison for you in my being.
Your freedom keeps you for me.
I'll release it again, and see
how it goes off, through sky,
through sea, through time, toward its destiny.
If that destiny is myself, it's waiting for you.

A ésa, a la que yo quiero,
no es a la que se da rindiéndose,
a la que se entrega cayendo,
de fatiga, de peso muerto,
como el agua por ley de lluvia,
hacia abajo, presa segura
de la tumba vaga del suelo.
A esa, a la que yo quiero,
es a la que se entrega venciendo,
venciéndose,
desde su libertad saltando
por el ímpetu de la gana,
de la gana de amor, surtida,
surtidor, o garza volante,
o disparada —la saeta—
sobre su pena victoriosa,
hacia arriba, ganando el cielo.

The one I love
doesn't give herself in surrender,
doesn't yield and fall,
from fatigue, from dead weight,
as water falls by the law of rain,
downward, certain prey
of the obscure grave of the soil.
The one I love
gives herself as a conqueror,
conquering herself,
leaping from her freedom
impelled by desire,
desire for love, gushing forth,
a fountain, or heron flying,
or sprung—the arrow—
victorious over her pain,
upward, reaching the sky.

¿Cómo me vas a explicar,
di, la dicha de esta tarde,
si no sabemos porqué
fue, ni cómo, ni de qué
ha sido,
si es pura dicha de nada?
En nuestros ojos visiones,
visiones y no miradas,
no percibían tamaños,
datos, colores, distancias.
De tan desprendidamente
como estaba yo y me estabas
mirando, más que mirando,
mis miradas te soñaban,
y me soñaban las tuyas.
Palabras sueltas, palabras,
deleite en incoherencias,
no eran ya signo de cosas,
eran voces puras, voces
de su servir olvidadas.
¡Cómo vagaron sin rumbo,
y sin torpeza, caricias!
Largos goces iniciados,
caricias no terminadas,
como si aun no se supiera
en qué lugar de los cuerpos

Tell me, how can you explain
the happiness of this afternoon,
if we don't know why
it was, or how, or what
caused it,
if it's sheer happiness of nothing?
In our eyes, visions—
visions and not glances—
perceived no dimensions,
facts, colors, distances.
I was feeling
so released, and you were gazing
at me, more than gazing—
my gaze was dreaming you,
and yours was dreaming me.
Words disconnected, words,
delight in incoherences,
were no longer signs of things,
they were pure voices, voices
that had forgotten their use.
How caresses roamed around without bearings
and without clumsiness.
Long delights begun,
caresses unfinished,
as if we didn't know yet
on which place of the body

el acariciar se acaba,
y anduviéramos buscándolo,
en lento encanto, sin ansia.
Las manos, no era tocar
lo que hacían en nosotros,
era descubrir; los tactos,
nuestros cuerpos inventaban,
allí en plena luz, tan claros
como en la plena tiniebla,
en donde sólo ellos pueden
ver los cuerpos,
con las ardorosas palmas.
Y de estas nadas se ha ido
fabricando, indestructible,
nuestra dicha, nuestro amor,
nuestra tarde.
Por eso aunque no fue nada,
sé que esta noche reclinas
lo mismo que una mejilla
sobre ese blancor de plumas
—almohada que ha sido alas—,
tu ser, tu memoria, todo,
y que todo te descansa,
sobre una tarde de dos,
que no es nada, nada, nada.

caressing ends,
and we were going about looking for it,
in slow enchantment, without urgency.
What our hands were doing to each other
was not touching,
but discovering; the contacts
were inventing our bodies,
there in full light, as clear
as in full darkness,
where only they,
with their burning palms,
can see bodies.
And from these nothings
our happiness, our love,
our afternoon was being
created, indestructibly.
That's why, though it was nothing,
I know tonight you're lying
as a cheek lies
upon that whiteness of feathers—
pillow which was wings—
your being, your memory, everything,
and that everything gives you repose,
upon an afternoon of two,
which is nothing, nothing, nothing.

La noche es la gran duda
del mundo y de tu amor.
Necesito que el día
cada día me diga
que es el día, que es él,
que es la luz: y allí tú.
Ese enorme hundimiento
de mármoles y cañas,
ese gran despintarse
del ala y de la flor:
la noche; la amenaza
ya de una abolición
del color y de ti,
me hace temblar: ¿la nada?
¿Me quisiste una vez?
Y mientras tú te callas
y es de noche, no sé
si luz, amor existen.
Necesito el milagro
insólito: otro día
y tu voz, confirmándome
el prodigio de siempre.
Y aunque te calles tú,
en la enorme distancia,
la aurora, por lo menos,

Night is the deep questioning
of the world and of your love.
I need day
to tell me each day
that it's day, it really is,
that it's light: and you are there.
That vast sinking
of marble and reed,
that enormous fading
of wing and flower:
night. And with it the threat
that color and you
will be abolished,
makes me tremble: nothingness?
Did you once love me?
And as long as you keep silent,
and night continues, I don't know
if light and love exist.
I need the special
miracle: another day,
and your voice confirming for me
the perennial marvel.
And even though you keep silent,
in the immense distance
there's dawn, at least,

la aurora, sí. La luz
que ella me traiga hoy
será el gran sí del mundo
al amor que te tengo.

dawn, yes. The light
it brings me today
will be the great yes of the world
to the love I feel for you.

Aquí
en esta orilla blanca
del lecho donde duermes
estoy al borde mismo
de tu sueño. Si diera
un paso más, caería
en sus ondas, rompiéndolo
como un cristal. Me sube
el calor de tu sueño
hasta el rostro. Tu hálito
te mide la andadura
del soñar: va despacio.
Un soplo alterno, leve
me entrega ese tesoro
exactamente: el ritmo
de tu vivir soñando.
Miro. Veo la estofa
de que está hecho tu sueño.
La tienes sobre el cuerpo
como coraza ingrávida.
Te cerca de respeto.
A tu virgen te vuelves
toda entera, desnuda,
cuando te vas al sueño.
En la orilla se paran
las ansias y los besos:

Here
on this white shore
of the bed where you're sleeping
I'm at the very edge
of your dream. If I took
one step more, I'd fall
into its waves, breaking it
like a crystal. The warmth
of your dream rises
to my face. Your breathing
measures the pace
of your dreaming: it goes slowly.
An alternating light breath
delivers that treasure to me
precisely: the rhythm
of your life as you dream.
I gaze. I see the stuff
of which your dream is made.
You hold it on your body
like a weightless armor.
It surrounds you with deference.
You become your virgin self,
entirely perfect, naked,
when you start off to the dream.
On the shore, desires
and kisses come to a halt:

esperan, ya sin prisa,
a que abriendo los ojos
renuncies a tu ser
invulnerable. Busco
tu sueño. Con mi alma
doblada sobre ti
las miradas recorren,
traslúcida, tu carne
y apartan dulcemente
las señas corporales,
por ver sí hallan detrás
las formas de tu sueño.
No lo encuentran. Y entonces
pienso en tu sueño. Quiero
descifrarlo. Las cifras
no sirven, no es secreto.
Es sueño y no misterio.
Y de pronto, en el alto
silencio de la noche,
un soñar mío empieza
al borde de tu cuerpo;
en él el tuyo siento.
Tú dormida, yo en vela,
hacíamos lo mismo.
No había que buscar:
tu sueño era mi sueño.

they wait, in no hurry now,
for you to open your eyes
and surrender your invulnerable
being. I'm searching
for your dream. With my soul
bent over you,
my glances move across
your translucent flesh
and gently turn aside
the corporeal signs,
trying to discover behind them
the forms of your dream.
They don't find them. And then
I think about your dream. I want
to decipher it. Ciphers
are of no use, it's not a secret.
It's a dream, and not a mystery.
And suddenly, in the deep
silence of night,
my own dreaming begins
at the edge of your body;
in my dreaming I feel yours.
You asleep, I awake,
we were doing the same thing.
No need to search:
your dream was my dream.

PART III

Qué alegría, vivir
sintiéndose vivido.
Rendirse
a la gran certidumbre, oscuramente,
de que otro ser, fuera de mí, muy lejos,
me está viviendo.
Que cuando los espejos, los espías,
azogues, almas cortas, aseguran
que estoy aquí, yo, inmóvil,
con los ojos cerrados y, los labios,
negándome al amor
de la luz, de la flor y de los nombres,
la verdad trasvisible es que camino
sin mis pasos, con otros,
allá lejos, y allí
estoy besando flores, luces, hablo.
Que hay otro ser por el que miro el mundo
porque me está queriendo con sus ojos.
Que hay otra voz con la que digo cosas
no sospechadas por mi gran silencio;
y es que también me quiere con su voz.
La vida—¡qué transporte ya!—, ignorancia
de lo que son mis actos, que ella hace,
en que ella vive, doble, suya y mía.
Y cuando ella me hable
de un cielo oscuro, de un paisaje blanco,

What joy to live
feeling lived.
To yield
to the deep certainty, darkly,
that another creature, outside me, far away,
is living me.
That when mirrors, spies,
reflections, pinched souls assert
that I'm here, motionless,
with eyes and lips closed,
denying myself to the love
of light, of flower and of names:
the transparent truth is, I move
not on my own footsteps but on others
far from here, and in that place
I'm kissing flowers, lights, I'm speaking.
There's another creature through whom I view the world
because she loves me with her eyes.
There's another voice with which I say things
unsuspected in my deep silence:
and it's because she loves me with her voice, as well.
Life—what transport!—not knowing
of my actions that she's performing:
double life in which she's living her own and mine.
And when she speaks to me
of a dark sky, of a white landscape,

recordaré
estrellas que no vi, que ella miraba,
y nieve que nevaba allá en su cielo.
Con la extraña delicia de acordarse
de haber tocado lo que no toqué
sino con esas manos que no alcanzo
a coger con las mías, tan distantes.
Y todo enajenado podrá el cuerpo
descansar, quieto, muerto ya. Morirse
en la alta confianza
de que este vivir mío no era sólo
mi vivir: era el nuestro. Y que me vive
otro ser por detrás de la no muerte.

I'll remember
stars I didn't see that she was looking at,
and snow that was snowing up there in her sky.
With the strange thrill of recalling
the touch of what I never touched
except with those hands I can't reach
to grasp in mine, they're so far away.
And utterly transported, my body
will be able to rest, quiet, dead, even. **Dying**
in complete confidence
that my life was not only
mine: it was ours. And that another
being is living me back of the nondeath.

¡Sensación de retorno!
Pero ¿de dónde, dónde?
Allí estuvimos, sí,
juntos. Para encontrarnos
este día tan claro
las presencias de siempre
no bastaban. Los besos
se quedaban a medio
vivir de sus destinos:
no sabían volar
de su ser en las bocas
hacia su pleno más.
Mi mirada, mirándote,
sentía paraísos
guardados más allá,
virginales jardines
de ti, donde con esta
luz de que disponíamos
no se podía entrar.

Por eso nos marchamos.
Se deshizo el abrazo,
se apartaron los ojos,
dejaron de mirarse
para buscar el mundo
donde nos encontráramos.

Sensation of returning!
But from where, where?
We were there, yes,
together. For us to meet
on this shining day,
the usual presences
weren't enough. Kisses
only half
lived out their destinies:
they couldn't fly
from the mouths where they existed
toward deeper fulfillment.
My gaze, gazing at you,
sensed paradises
preserved further away,
virginal gardens
of yours where
we couldn't enter
with this light at our disposal.

That's why we went away.
Our embrace unbound itself,
our eyes withdrew,
stopped gazing at each other
in order to search for the world
where we had met.

Y ha sido allí, sí, allí.
Nos hemos encontrado
allí. ¿Cómo, el encuentro?
¿Fue como beso o llanto?
¿Nos hallamos
con las manos, buscándonos
a tientas, con los gritos,
clamando, con las bocas
que el vacío besaban?
¿Fue un choque de materia
y materia, combate
de pecho contra pecho,
que a fuerza de contactos
se convirtió en victoria
gozosa de los dos,
en prodigioso pacto
de tu ser con mi ser
enteros?
¿O tan sencillo fue,
tan sin esfuerzo, como
una luz que se encuentra
con otra luz, y queda
iluminado el mundo,
sin que nada se toque?
Ninguno lo sabemos.
Ni el dónde. Aquí en las manos,
como las cicatrices,
allí, dentro del alma,
como un alma del alma,
pervive el prodigioso
saber que nos hallamos,
y que su donde está

And it happened there, yes, there.
We found each other
there. What was it like, that meeting?
Was it like a kiss or tears?
Did we find each other
with our hands, groping
for each other, with cries,
calling out, with mouths
kissing empty space?
Was it a clash of substance
and substance, struggle
of breast against breast,
which by force of contact
was transformed into joyous
victory for both,
into the miraculous covenant
of your whole being
and my whole being?
Or was it as simple,
as effortless,
as a light that meets
another light: and the world
is illuminated,
though nothing is touched?
Neither of us knows what
or where. Here in our hands,
like scars,
and there in our souls,
like a soul of the soul
the marvelous knowledge persists
that we found each other,
and that the *where*

para siempre cerrado.
Ha sido tan hermoso
que no sufre memoria,
como sufren las fechas
los nombres o las líneas.
Nada en ese milagro
podría ser recuerdo:
porque el recuerdo es
la pena de sí mismo,
el dolor del tamaño,
del tiempo, y todo fue
eternidad: relámpago.
Si quieres recordarlo
no sirve el recordar.
Sólo vale vivir
de cara hacia ese donde,
queriéndolo, buscándolo.

is closed forever.
It was so beautiful
it can't be recalled
like dates,
names or lines.
Nothing in that miracle
could be a memory:
because memory is
the sorrow of self,
the pain of size,
of time. And everything was
eternity: a lightning-flash.
If you want to recall it,
remembering won't help.
You can only live
facing toward that *where,*
desiring it, seeking it.

De noche la distancia
parece sólo oscuridad, tiniebla
que no separa sino por los ojos.
El mundo se ha apagado,
pasajera avería del gozo de mirarse;
pero todo
lo que se quiere cerca,
está al alcance del querer, cerquísima,
como está el ser amado, cuando está
su respirar, el ritmo de su cuerpo,
al lado nuestro, aunque sin verse.
Se sueña
que en la esperanza del silencio oscuro
nada nos falta, y que a la luz primera
los labios y los ojos y la voz
encontrarán sus términos ansiados:
otra voz, otros ojos, otros labios.

Y amanece el error. La luz separa.
Alargando las manos no se alcanza
el cuerpo de la dicha, que en la noche
tendido se sentía junto al nuestro,
sin prisa por trocarlo en paraíso:
sólo se palpan soledades nuevas,
ofertas de la luz. Y la distancia
es distancia, son leguas, años, cielos;

In the night, distance
seems only dimness, darkness
that causes no separation except through the eyes.
The world has faded away,
for a while damaging the joy of looking at each other:
but everything
that's desired close by,
lies within reach of the desiring, very close by,
as does the beloved person
when her breathing, the rhythm of her body,
is there beside us, even though not seen.
One dreams
that in the dark hopeful silence
nothing is missing, and that at the first light,
lips and eyes and voice
will find their desired ends:
another voice, other eyes, other lips.

And the error dawns. Light separates.
Stretching out our hands, we don't reach
the body of happiness which during the night
we felt lying beside ours,
in no hurry to change it into paradise:
only new solitudes are touched,
offered by the light. And the distance
is distance, it's leagues, years, skies;

es la luz, la distancia. Y hay que andarla,
andar pisando luz, horas y horas,
para que nuestro paso, al fin del día,
gane la orilla oscura
en que cesan las pruebas de estar solo.
Donde el querer, en la tiniebla, piensa
que con decir un nombre
una felicidad contestaría.
Y cuando en la honda noche se nos colman
con júbilos, con besos o con muertes,
los anhelosos huecos,
que amor y luz abrieron en las almas.

it's light, distance is. And we have to walk it,
walk treading the light, for hours and hours,
so that our step, at day's end,
may reach the dark shore
on which cease the trials of being alone.
Where love, in the darkness, thinks
that if one said a name,
a happiness would answer.
And when in the depth of night
rejoicings, kisses, or deaths
fill the yearning spaces for us
which love and light opened in our souls.

A veces un no niega
más de lo que quería, se hace múltiple.
Se dice "no, no iré"
y se destejen infinitas tramas
tejidas por los síes lentamente,
se niegan las promesas que no nos hizo nadie
sino nosotros mismos, al oído.
Cada minuto breve rehusado,
—¿eran quince, eran treinta?—
se dilata en sin fines, se hace siglos,
y un "no, esta noche no"
puede negar la eternidad de noches,
la pura eternidad.
¡Qué difícil saber adonde hiere
un no! Inocentemente
sale de labios puros, un no puro;
sin mancha ni querencia
de herir, va por el aire.
Pero el aire está lleno
de esperanzas en vuelo, las encuentra
y las traspasa por las alas tiernas
su inmensa fuerza ciega, sin querer,
y las deja sin vida y va a clavarse
en ese techo azul que nos pintamos
y abre una grieta allí.
O allí rebota

At times a "no" denies
more than it meant to, becomes multiple.
One says, "No, I'm not going"
and infinite wefts ravel
that were woven gradually by the "yeses,"
promises are denied which no one made us
except ourselves, in our ear.
Each brief minute rejected—
was it fifteen, was it thirty?—
swells into forevers, becomes centuries,
and a "no, not tonight"
can deny the eternity of nights,
pure eternity.
How difficult to know where a "no"
will strike! Innocently
it comes from pure lips, a pure "no";
untainted, not wanting
to wound, it goes through the air.
But the air is full
of hopes in flight, the "no" runs into them
and drives its immense blind force
through the delicate wings, without meaning to,
and leaves them lifeless and proceeds to thrust
into that blue ceiling which we imagine,
and opens up a crack there.
Or rebounds from there,

y su herir acerado
vuelve camino atrás y le desgarra
el pecho, al mismo pecho que lo dijo.
Un no da miedo. Hay que dejarlo siempre
al borde de los labios y dudarlo.
O decirlo tan suavemente
que le llegue
al que no lo esperaba
con un sonar de "sí",
aunque no dijo sí quién lo decía.

and its piercing steel
turns back in passage and rends
the breast, the same breast that spoke the word.
A "no" is fearful. We must always leave it
at the edge of our lips and question it.
Or speak so gently
that it comes
to the one who wasn't expecting it
with the sound of "yes,"
even though it wasn't "yes" that was said.

Ahora te quiero,
como el mar quiere a su agua:
desde fuera, por arriba,
haciéndose sin parar
con ella tormentas, fugas,
albergues, descansos, calmas.
¡Qué frenesíes, quererte!
¡Qué entusiasmo de olas altas,
y qué desmayos de espuma
van y vienen! Un tropel
de formas, hechas, deshechas,
galopan desmelenadas.
Pero detrás de sus flancos
está soñándose un sueño
de otra forma más profunda
de querer, que está allá abajo:
de no ser ya movimiento,
de acabar este vaivén,
este ir y venir, de cielos
a abismos, de hallar por fin
la inmóvil flor sin otoño
de un quererse quieto, quieto.
Más allá de ola y espuma
el querer busca su fondo.
Esa hondura donde el mar
hizo la paz con su agua

Now I love you
as the sea loves its water:
from outside, from above,
endlessly creating with it
storms, escapes,
shelters, pauses, calms.
What frenzy, loving you!
What rapture of high waves,
and what swirling of foam
are coming and going! A jumble
of forms, created, destroyed,
gallop about disheveled.
But behind their flanks
a dream is being dreamed
of another, deeper form
of loving, far down below:
of no longer being movement,
of ceasing this coming and going,
this going and coming, from heaven
to the abyss, of finding at last
the motionless flower with no autumn,
flower of loving each other in stillness, stillness.
Beyond wave and spray
love seeks its depth.
That bottom where the sea
made peace with its water;

y están queriéndose ya
sin signo, sin movimiento.
Amor
tan sepultado en su ser,
tan entregado, tan quieto,
que nuestro querer en vida
se sintiese
seguro de no acabar
cuando terminan los besos,
las miradas, las señales.
Tan cierto de no morir
como está
el gran amor de los muertos.

and they're loving each other now
without a sign, without a motion.
Love
so buried in its being,
so surrendered, so still,
that our love during life
would feel
certain of never ending
when kisses end,
and gazes, and pledges.
As certain of not dying
as the deep
love of the dead.

Nadadora de noche, nadadora
entre olas y tinieblas.
Brazos blancos hundiéndose, naciendo,
con un ritmo
regido por designios ignorados,
avanzas
contra la doble resistencia sorda
de oscuridad y mar, de mundo oscuro.
Al naufragar el día,
tú, pasajera
de travesías por abril y mayo,
te quisiste salvar, te estás salvando,
de la resignación, no de la muerte.
Se te rompen las olas, desbravadas,
hecho su asombro espuma,
arrepentidas ya de su milicia,
cuando tú les ofreces, como un pacto,
tu fuerte pecho virgen.
Se te rompen
las densas ondas anchas de la noche
contra ese afán de claridad que buscas,
brazada por brazada, y que levanta
un espumar altísimo en el cielo;
espumas de luceros, sí, de estrellas,
que te salpica el rostro
con un tumulto de constelaciones,

Night swimmer, swimmer
through waves and darkness.
White arms submerging, emerging,
with a rhythm
directed by designs unknown:
you advance
against twofold silent resistance—
of sea's darkness, of the dark world.
When day shipwrecks,
you, voyager
crossing through April and May,
you tried to save yourself, you're saving yourself,
from resignation, not from death.
Waves break over you, and are tamed:
their amazement turned to foam,
regretting their warfare now
when you offer them
your firm virgin breast as a covenant.
The dense wide waves
of night break against you,
against your longing and seeking for clarity,
armful by armful, as it raises
towering foam to the sky:
foam of day-stars, yes, of night-stars,
spattering your face
with a tumult of constellations,

de mundos. Desafía
mares de siglos, siglos de tinieblas,
tu inocencia desnuda.
Y el rítmico ejercicio de tu cuerpo
soporta, empuja, salva
mucho más que tu carne, Así tu triunfo
tu fin será, y al cabo, traspasadas
el mar, la noche, las conformidades,
del otro lado ya del mundo negro,
en la playa del día que alborea,
morirás en la aurora que ganaste.

of worlds. Your naked innocence
challenges the seas of centuries,
centuries of darkness.
And the rhythmic movement of your body
supports, impels, rescues
much more than your flesh. Thus your triumph
will be your end; and having finally passed beyond
sea, night, compliances,
on the other side of the black world now,
on the shore where day is breaking,
you'll die in the dawn you attained.

¿Serás, amor,
un largo adiós que no se acaba?
Vivir, desde el principio, es separarse.
En el primer encuentro
con la luz, con los labios,
el corazón percibe la congoja
de tener que estar ciego y solo un día.
Amor es el retraso milagroso
de su término mismo:
es prolongar el hecho mágico,
de que uno y uno sean dos, en contra
de la primer condena le la vida.
Con los besos,
con la pena y el pecho se conquistan,
en afanosas lides, entre gozos
parecidos a juegos,
días, tierras, espacios fabulosos,
a la gran disyunción que está esperando,
hermana de la muerte o muerte misma.
Cada beso perfecto aparta el tiempo,
le echa hacia atrás, ensancha el mundo breve
donde puede besarse todavía.
Ni en el llegar, ni en il hallazgo
tiene el amor su cima:
es en la resistencia a separarse
en donde se le siente,

Will you be, love,
a long, never-ending good-by?
Right from the start, living means leaving each other.
In the first encounter
with light, with lips,
the heart feels the anguish
of having to be blind and alone, one day.
Love is the miraculous postponement
of its own ending:
prolonging the magic fact
that one and one make two, in contradiction
of the first penalty of life.
With kisses,
with suffering and courage,
in hard contests, among pleasures
resembling games:
days, earths, fabulous spaces are won over
from the enormous disjoining that awaits us,
sister of death or death itself.
Every perfect kiss dissuades time,
pushes it back, extends the brief world
where kisses are still possible.
Love reaches its summit
neither in arrival nor in discovery
but in resisting separation
where it feels

desnudo, altísimo, temblando.
Y la separación no es el momento
cuando brazos, o voces,
se despiden con señas materiales.
Es de antes, de después.
Si se estrechan las manos, si se abraza,
nunca es para apartarse,
es porque el alma ciegamente siente
que la forma posible de estar juntos
es una despedida larga, clara.
Y que lo más seguro es el adiós.

naked, sublime, tremulous.
Nor is separation the moment
when arms or voices
bid good-by with physical gestures.
It's before, and after.
Hands clasp, bodies embrace:
not in order to pull apart, ever,
but because the spirit blindly feels
the only way to stay together
is a long, clear leave-taking.
And the deepest certainty is good-by.

Tarde afilada y seca
corta como un cuchillo.
¡Unidad de mi alma!

En un siempre se hinca:
el tiempo, que era un siempre,
partido: ayer, mañana.
Y aquella sombra sola,
única, por la arena,
truncada en dos: tú y yo.

Secos rasgos, los vientos
firman sentencias últimas
de setiembre, destinos.
Aquí el tuyo, allí el mío.

Adioses, sin adiós,
ni pañuelo. El acero
del otoño la vida
nos parte en dos mitades.
La vida
toda entera, dorada,
redonda, allí colgando
en la rama de agosto
donde tú la cogiste.

Afternoon, tapering and dry,
cuts like a knife.
Oneness of my soul!

It thrusts into an always:
time, which was an always,
divided: yesterday, tomorrow.
And that solitary shadow,
the single one, on the sand,
slashed in two: you and me.

With dry strokes, the winds
sign the fatal verdicts
of September, destinies.
Yours here, mine there.

Good-bys, without a good-by,
nor a handkerchief. The steel
of autumn divides
our life in two halves.
Life so whole, golden,
complete, hanging there
on the branch of August
where you gathered it.

No importa que no te tenga,
no importa que no te vea.
Antes te abrazaba,
antes te miraba,
te buscaba toda,
te quería entera.
Hoy ya no les pido,
ni a manos ni a ojos,
las últimas pruebas.
Estar a mi lado
te pedía antes;
sí, junto a mí, sí,
sí, pero allí fuera.
Y me contentaba
sentir que tus manos
me daban tus manos,
sentir que a mis ojos
les dabas presencia.
Lo que ahora te pido
es más, mucho más,
que beso o mirada:
es que estés más cerca
de mí mismo, dentro.
Como el viento está
invisible, dando
su vida a la vela.

No matter I'm not holding you,
no matter I'm not seeing you.
A while ago I was embracing you,
a while ago I was gazing at you,
searching for you, all of you,
I loved the whole of you.
Today I no longer ask
either your hands or your eyes
for ultimate proofs.
Be here at my side,
I'd ask you in those days:
yes, close to me, yes,
yes, but there outside me.
And I was content
to feel that your hands
were giving me your hands,
to feel you giving
your presence to my eyes.
What I ask you for now
is more, much more,
than a kiss or a look:
it's that you be closer
to the self of me, inside.
As the wind is
invisible, giving
its life to the candle.

Como está la luz
quieta, fija, inmóvil,
sirviendo de centro
que nunca vacila
al trémulo cuerpo
de llama que tiembla.
Como está la estrella,
presente y segura,
sin voz y sin tacto,
en el pecho abierto,
sereno, del lago.
Lo que yo te pido
es sólo que seas
alma de mi ánima,
sangre de mi sangre
dentro de las venas.
Es que estés en mí
como el corazón
mío que jamás
veré, tocaré,
y cuyos latidos
no se cansan nunca
de darme mi vida
hasta que me muera.
Como el esqueleto,
el secreto hondo
de mi ser, que sólo
me verá la tierra,
pero que en el mundo
es el que se encarga
de llevar mi peso
de carne y de sueño,
de gozo y de pena

As light is still,
fixed, unmoving,
serving as a never-
wavering center
for the tremulous body
of the quivering flame.
As the star lies,
present and secure,
without voice or touch,
on the open, serene
breast of the lake.
What I ask of you
is only that you be
soul of my soul,
blood of my blood
flowing in my veins.
That you exist in me
as my own heart
which I shall never see,
shall never touch,
and whose pulsations
do not tire, ever,
of giving me life
until I die.
As the skeleton,
the profound secret
of my being, which only
earth shall see of me,
but which, in the world,
is what charges itself
with bearing my weight
of flesh and of dream,
of joy and of sorrow

misteriosamente
sin que haya unos ojos
que jamás le vean.
Lo que yo te pido
es que la corpórea
pasajera ausencia
no nos sea olvido,
ni fuga, ni falta:
sino que me sea
posesión total
del alma lejana,
eterna presencia.

mysteriously
without ever being seen
by any eyes.
What I ask of you
is that the body's
transitory absence
may not be oblivion for us,
nor flight, nor emptiness:
but may be for me
total possession
of the distant spirit,
timeless presence.

No quiero que te vayas,
dolor, última forma
de amar. Me estoy sintiendo
vivir cuando me dueles
no en ti, ni aquí, más lejos:
en la tierra, en el año
de donde vienes tú,
en el amor con ella
y todo lo que fue.
En esa realidad
hundida que se niega
a sí misma y se empeña
en que nunca ha existido,
que sólo fue un pretexto
mío para vivir.
Si tú no me quedaras,
dolor, irrefutable,
yo me lo creería;
pero me quedas tú.
Tu verdad me asegura
que nada fue mentira.
Y mientras yo te sienta,
tú me serás, dolor,
la prueba de otra vida
en que no me dolías.

I don't want you to go away,
pain, ultimate form
of loving. I feel
myself living when you make me suffer,
not in you, not here, but far off:
in the land, in the year
you come from,
in the love we had
and all that was.
In that shattered
reality which disowns
itself and insists
it has never existed,
that it was only a pretext
of mine for living.
If you weren't still with me,
undeniable pain—
I'd come to believe it;
but you're still with me.
Your reality convinces me
none of it was invented.
And as long as I feel you,
pain, you'll be
my proof of another life
in which you didn't make me suffer.

La gran prueba, a lo lejos,
de que existió, que existe,
de que me quiso, sí,
de que aún la estoy queriendo.

The deep proof, at a distance,
that she existed, that she lives,
that she loved me, yes,
that I'm still in love with her.

Me estoy labrando tu sombra.
La tengo ya sin los labios,
rojos y duros: ardían.
Te los habría besado
aún mucho más.

Luego te paro los brazos,
rápidos, largos, nerviosos.
Me ofrecían el camino
para que yo te estrechara.

Te arranco el color, el bulto.
Te mato el paso. Venías
derecha a mí. Lo que más
pena me ha dado, al callártela,
es tu voz. Densa, tan cálida,
más palpable que tu cuerpo.
Pero ya iba a traicionarnos.

Así
mi amor está libre, suelto,
con tu sombra descarnada.
Y puedo vivir en ti
sin temor
a lo que yo más deseo,
a tu beso, a tus abrazos.

I'm forming your shadow for myself.
I've got it already, except for the lips,
red and firm: they used to burn.
I'd have kissed them
much more, even.

Then I immobilize your arms,
swift, long, nervous.
They used to offer me the way
to hold you close.

I rub out your color, your bulk.
I destroy your step. You used to come
straight toward me. What's made me
suffer most, silencing it,
is your voice. Rich, ardent,
more palpable than your body.
But it was going to betray us in the end.

In this way,
my love is free, released,
with your shadow stripped of flesh.
And I can live in you
without fear
of what I most desire:
your kiss, your arms.

Estar ya siempre pensando
en los labios, en la voz,
en el cuerpo,
que yo mismo te arranqué
para poder, ya sin ellos,
quererte.
¡Yo, que los quería tanto!
Y estrechar sin fin, sin pena
—mientras se va inasidera,
con mi gran amor detrás,
la carne por su camino—
tu solo cuerpo posible:
tu dulce cuerpo pensado.

Can be thinking always
of your lips, of your voice,
of your body
which I myself ripped away from you
so I might, without them now
love you.
I who loved them so much!
And hold close forever, without pain—
while that flesh, not to be grasped,
goes on its way,
with my deep love following—
your only possible body:
your sweet body in my thoughts.

Sí, tú naciste al borrárseme
tu forma.
Mientras yo te recordé
¡qué muerta estabas!
tan terminada en tus lindes.
Se te podía seguir
como en un mapa, clarísima,
al norte
la voz seca, boreal,
tibia, abandonada, al sur,
en litoral, la sonrisa.
Tú vivías, suficiente,
en tu color, en tus gestos,
encerrada entre medidas.

Pero un día de noviembre
dejaste en blanco tus atlas,
se abolieron tus fronteras,
te escapaste del recuerdo.
Estabas ya, sin tus límites,
perdida en la desmemoria.
Y te tuve que inventar
—era en el segundo día—
nueva,
con tu voz o sin tu voz,
con tu carne o sin tu carne.

Yes, yes, you were born when your form
was erased from me.
While I remembered you,
how dead you were,
so finished in your boundaries!
One could follow you,
most clear, like a map:
to the north
your voice, dry, boreal;
to the south, on the coastline,
your smile, warm, surrendering.
You lived self-sufficient
in your color, your gestures,
locked up within measurements.

But one November day
you left your atlases blank,
your borders were abolished,
you escaped from memory.
Without your limits
you were already lost in oblivion.
And I had to invent you—
it was on the second day—
anew,
with your voice or without your voice,
with your flesh or without your flesh.

Daba lo mismo.
Eras ya de mí, incapaz
de vivirte ya sin mí.
A mis medidas de dentro
te fui inventando, Afrodita,
perfecta de entre el olvido,
virgen y nueva, surgida
del olvido de tu forma.

It was all the same.
You were now mine, unable
to exist any longer without me.
according to my inner specifications
I kept inventing you, Aphrodite,
perfected out of forgetting,
virgin and new, arisen
from the forgetting of your form.

Pensar en ti esta noche
no era pensarte con mi pensamiento,
yo solo, desde mí. Te iba pensando
conmigo extensamente, el ancho mundo.

El gran sueño del campo, las estrellas,
callado el mar, las hierbas invisibles,
sólo presentes en perfumes secos,
todo,
de Aldebarán al grillo te pensaba.

¡Qué sosegadamente
se hacía la concordia
entre las piedras, los luceros,
el agua muda, la arboleda trémula,
todo lo inanimado,
y el alma mía
dedicándolo a ti! Todo acudía
dócil a mi llamada, a tu servicio,
ascendido a intención y a fuerza amante.
Concurrían las luces y las sombras
a la luz de quererte; concurrían
el gran silencio, por la tierra, plano,
suaves voces de nube, por el cielo,
al cántico hacia ti que en mí cantaba.
Una conformidad de mundo y ser,

Thinking of you tonight
I wasn't thinking you with my thought,
I alone, from myself. The wide world,
far and near, was thinking you with me.

The immense dream of the countryside, the stars,
the sea keeping silent, the grasses invisible,
present only in dry perfumes,
everything,
from Aldebaran to the cricket was thinking of you.

How serenely
harmony grew
between stones, stars,
mute water, tremulous grove,
all inanimate things,
and my soul
dedicating them to you! Everything was responding
gently to my call, in your service,
risen to purpose and loving strength.
Lights and shadows were gathering
to the light of loving you; gathering
was the vast level silence, on earth,
soft cloud voices, across the sky,
in the canticle to you that sang in me.
An agreement of world and being,

de afán y tiempo, inverosímil tregua,
se entraba en mí, como la dicha entra
cuando llega sin prisa, beso a beso.
Y casi
dejé de amarte por amarte más,
en más que en mí, confiando inmensamente
ese empleo de amar a la gran noche
errante por el tiempo y ya cargada
de misión, misionera
de un amor vuelto estrellas, calma, mundo,
salvado ya del miedo
al cadáver que queda si se olvida.

of desire and time, improbable truce,
entered me, as happiness enters,
when it comes without haste, kiss by kiss.
And I almost
stopped loving you for loving you more,
in more than myself, deeply entrusting
that use of loving to the immense night
wandering through time, and now charged
with a mission: emissary
of a love become stars, stillness, world,
saved now from the fear
of the corpse that's left if we forget.

Hoy son las manos la memoria.
El alma no se acuerda, está dolida
de tanto recordar. Pero en las manos
queda el recuerdo de lo que han tenido.

Recuerdo de una piedra
que hubo junto a un arroyo
y que cogimos distraídamente
sin darnos cuenta de nuestra ventura.
Pero su peso áspero,
sentir nos hace que por fin cogimos
el fruto más hermoso de los tiempos.
A tiempo sabe
el peso de una piedra entre las manos.
En una piedra está
la paciencia del mundo, madurada despacio.
Incalulable suma
de días y de noches, sol y agua
la que costó esta forma torpe y dura
que acariciar no sabe y acompaña
tan sólo con su peso, oscuramente.
Se estuvo siempre quieta,
sin buscar, encerrada,
en una voluntad densa y constante
de no volar como la mariposa,
de no ser bella, como el lirio,

Today my hands are my memory.
My soul doesn't remember, it aches
from so much remembering. But in my hands
remains the recollection of what they've held.

Recollection of a stone
which was lying beside a stream,
and which we picked up carelessly,
without realizing our good fortune.
But its harsh weight
makes us feel we finally gathered
the handsomest fruit of the centuries.
The weight of a stone in the hands
tastes of time.
In a stone lies
the patience of the world, slowly ripened.
Incalculable sum
of days and of nights, sun and water
required to make this torpid, heavy form
that can't give caresses, and that's present
with its weight alone, darkly.
To preserve its purity from envy,
it stayed forever still,
never seeking anything, enclosed,
in a dense and persistent will
not to soar like the butterfly,
nor be beautiful, like the lily.

para salvar de envidias su pureza.
¡Cuántos esbeltos lirios, cuántas gráciles
libélulas se han muerto, allí, a su lado
por correr tanto hacia la primavera!
Ella supo esperar sin pedir nada
más que la eternidad de su ser puro.
Por renunciar al pétalo, y al vuelo,
está viva y me enseña
que un amor debe estarse quizá quieto, muy quieto,
soltar las falsas alas de la prisa,
y derrotar así su propia muerte.

También recuerdan ellas, mis manos,
haber tenido una cabeza amada entre sus palmas.
Nada más misterioso en este mundo.
Los dedos reconocen los cabellos
lentamente, uno a uno, como hojas
de calendario: son recuerdos
de otros tantos, también innumerables
días felices,
dóciles al amor que los revive.
Pero al palpar la forma inexorable
que detrás de la carne nos resiste
las palmas ya se quedan ciegas.
No son caricias, no, lo que repiten
pasando y repasando sobre el hueso:
son preguntas sin fin, son infinitas
angustias hechas tactos ardorosos.
Y nada les contesta: una sospecha
de que todo se escapa y se nos huye
cuando entre nuestras manos lo oprimimos
nos sube del calor de aquella frente.
La cabeza se entrega. ¿Es la entrega absoluta?

How many slender lilies, how many graceful
dragonflies have died there beside it,
from rushing so toward spring!
The stone knew how to wait without asking for anything
more than the eternity of its pure being.
By renouncing petal, and flight,
it is still alive and teaches me
that a love should perhaps stay still, very still,
loosen the false wings of haste,
and defeat in this way its own death.

They also recall, these hands of mine,
having held a loved head between their palms.
Nothing more mysterious in this world.
Fingers examine the hair
slowly, one strand at a time, like pages
of a calendar: they're reminders
of many other days, countless
and happy as they were—
yielding to the love which relives them again.
But feeling the relentless form
that resists us behind the flesh,
our palms are now blinded.
It's not caresses, no, which they repeat,
passing and repassing over bone:
it's endless questions, it's infinite
anxieties turned into feverish probings.
And nothing answers them: a suspicion
reaches us from the warmth of that brow,
that everything vanishes and eludes us
when we press it between our hands.
The head surrenders: is the surrender complete?

El peso en nuestras manos lo insinúa,
los dedos se lo creen,
y quieren convencerse: palpan, palpan.
Pero una voz oscura tras la frente,
—¿nuestra frente o la suya?—
nos dice que el misterio más lejano,
porque está allí tan cerca, no se toca
con la carne mortal con que buscamos
allí, en la punta de los dedos,
la presencia invisible.
Teniendo una cabeza así cogida
nada se sabe, nada,
sino que está el futuro decidiendo
o nuestra vida o nuestra muerte,
tras esas pobres manos engañadas
por la hermosura de lo que sostienen.
Entre unas manos ciegas
que no pueden saber. Cuya fe única
está en ser buenas, en hacer caricias
sin cansarse, por ver si así se ganan
cuando ya la cabeza amada vuelva
a vivir otra vez sobre sus hombros,
y parezca que nada les queda entre las palmas,
el triunfo de no estar nunca vacías.

The weight in our hands suggests it,
our fingers believe it,
and want to convince themselves: they're probing, probing.
But a dark voice behind the forehead—
our forehead or its?—
tells us that the further mystery,
since it's there, so close by, can't be felt
by mortal flesh with which we're searching
there, at the tips of our fingers,
for the invisible presence.
Holding a head clasped that way
we know nothing, nothing
except that the future's deciding
either our life or our death,
back of these poor hands deceived
by the beauty of what they're holding.
Blind hands
unable to know. Whose only faith
lies in being good, in giving caresses
tirelessly, to see if in that way—
when the beloved head again returns
to live once more on its shoulders,
and nothing's left, apparently, between these palms—
they earn the triumph of never being empty.

De entre todas las cosas verticales
en que el mundo revela
su parecido con la llama, anhelo
de vivir hacia arriba o no vivir,
lo que yo ahora te ofrezco a la memoria
no son los delicados rascacielos
con túnicas a cuadros,
de luz y sombra, por la noche, coro
de lánguidos y esbeltos Arlequines
en el aire ambicioso de Manhattan.
No son las almas de pasadas ninfas
que a su inmortalidad han ascendido,
por fin, en los jardines disfrazándose
de surtidores, y que en estos cuerpos
nuevos y de cristal, ya traspasaron
las leyes de la carne y su fatiga
y eternizan la danza contra el tiempo
dando envidia a las flores que se cansan.
No las metálicas escalas
por donde suben bajo cascos épicos
los caprichos, vestidos de bomberos,
a salvar en el piso veinticuatro
de la más alta casa de muñecas
a algún alma cansada,
que se ha quedado allí
dormida por descuido, y sin salida.

Among all the vertical things
in which the world reveals
its resemblance to flame—that longing
to live upward or not live at all—
I'm not offering your memory now
delicate skyscrapers
with checked tunics
of light and shadow, by night, a choir
of languid slender harlequins
in the striving air of Manhattan.
Nor souls of nymphs of long ago
who've risen to their immortality,
at last, masquerading as garden
fountains; who already transcended,
in these new crystalline bodies,
the laws of flesh and its fatigue,
and endlessly prolong the dance against time—
causing envy among the drooping flowers.
Nor metal ladders
on which whims dressed as firemen
climb, under epic helmets,
to rescue on the twenty-fourth floor
of the highest doll-house,
some weary soul
who's remained there
heedlessly asleep, and without means of escape.

Ni es la palmera, ni es
la verticalidad que más nos duele,
la de estar solos, solos, solos, solos.
Rectos como los faros, apagados.
Porque la soledad es la absoluta,
vertical, ya sin luz, sin hojas, de este mundo.
No. Lo que te recuerdo
son dos voces. Dos voces, una noche,
de dos seres tendidos,
allí, en la misma cama.
Y hablaron: y sus cuerpos,
los derribados troncos
de donde ellas nacían,
seguían boca arriba, separados,
sin volverse uno a otro,
por no alterar la vertical pureza
de su paralelismo por el aire
oscuro de las tres de la mañana.
Se hablaban, sin mirarse,
como si aún estuvieran
inmensamente aparte, distanciados.
Los ojos esperaban,
ya todos preparados a su gozo,
si una luz encendía alguna mano:
mas nadie la encendió, los dos siguieron,
prefiriendo no verse.
Los labios y los brazos
en el umbral temblaban
del hermoso camino violento
que el cuerpo sigue tantas veces.
Y ninguno besó. La forma última
del amor, esa noche,
era estarse muy quietos, en lo oscuro,

Nor the palm tree, nor
that most painful verticality
of our being alone, alone, alone, alone.
Straight as lighthouses, extinguished.
For solitude is the absolute,
vertical—without light, even, without leaves—of the world.
No. I'm recalling two voices
to you. Two voices, one night,
of two persons stretched out,
there, on the same bed.
And they talked: and their bodies,
those prostrate trunks
from which the voices rose,
lay face up, apart,
without turning to each other,
lest they alter the vertical purity
of their parallelism in the dim
air of three in the morning.
They talked without looking at each other,
as though they were still
separated by an immense distance.
Their eyes were waiting,
quite ready to rejoice
if a beam kindled one of their hands:
but no one kindled it, the two stayed there,
choosing not to see each other.
Lips and arms
trembled on the threshold
of the beautiful violent course
the body takes so many times.
And neither kissed. The ultimate form
of love, that night,
was to lie very still, in darkness,

para fingir que ya tan sólo
dos limpias voces, puras, paralelas,
quedaban de sus vidas, de sus ansias.
Habitantes, por fin, del paraíso
donde sin pena o condición de carne,
de color o de nombre, de fecha o de sollozo,
las voces verticales
de los que tanto amaron torpemente,
echados, sobre el mundo,
puestas en pie, derechas
igual que llamas de su propia lumbre
traspasan las mortales fronteras
que de sí mismas arden, silenciosas,
se dicen lo que tienen que decirse
sin encender las luces de sus cuerpos.

simply pretending that now only two clear, pure,
parallel voices remained
from their lives, from their longings.
They live, at last, in paradise,
without distress or condition of flesh,
of color or of name, of date or of sobbing breath.
And the vertical voices
of those who loved so slowly,
stretched out upon the world—
rising up straight
as flames from their own fire,
cross the mortal frontiers
which of themselves are burning, silently.
And they tell each other what they must,
without kindling the fires of their bodies.

¿Las oyes cómo piden realidades,
ellas, desmelenadas, fieras,
ellas, los sombras que los dos forjamos
en este inmenso lecho de distancias?
Cansadas ya de infinitud, de tiempo
sin medida, de anónimo, heridas
por una gran nostalgia de materia,
piden límites, días, nombres.
No pueden
vivir así ya más: están al borde
del morir de las sombras, que es la nada.
Acude, ven, conmigo
Tiende tus manos, tiéndeles tu cuerpo.
Los dos les buscaremos
un color, una fecha, un pecho, un sol.
Que descansen en ti, sé tú su carne.
Se calmará su enorme ansia errante,
mientras las estrechamos
ávidamente entre los cuerpos nuestros
donde encuentren su pasto y su reposo.
Se dormirán al fin en nuestro sueño
abrazado, abrazadas. Y así luego,
al separarnos, al nutrirnos sólo
de sombras, entre lejos,
ellas
tendrán recuerdos ya, tendrán pasado

Do you hear how they're demanding realities,
these fierce disheveled
shadows we two forged together
in this immense bed of distances?
Weary now of infinity, of time
without measure, of anonymity, stricken
with a deep longing for physical substance,
they demand limits, days, names.
They can't
live this way any more: they're on the verge
of dying as shadows, which is nothingness.
Come join me.
Hold out your hands, hold out your body toward them.
Together we shall seek out for them
a color, a date, a breast, a sun.
Let them repose in you, you be their flesh.
Their terrible yearning to wander will calm down,
while we press them
fervently between our bodies
where they may find their nourishment and their rest.
Embraced, they'll fall asleep at last in our sleeping
embrace. And thus, later,
when we part, when we feed
on shadows alone, far away,
they
will have memories by then, they'll have a past

de carne y hueso,
el tiempo que vivieron en nosotros.
Y su afanoso sueño
de sombras, otra vez, será el retorno
a esta corporeidad mortal y rosa
donde el amor inventa su infinito.

of flesh and bone,
the time when they lived in us.
And their anxious sleep
of shadows will return once more
to this mortal rose-colored body
in which love creates its eternity.

No en palacios de mármol,
no en meses, no, ni en cifras,
nunca pisando el suelo:
en leves mundos frágiles
hemos vivido juntos.
El tiempo se contaba
apenas por minutos:
un minuto era un siglo,
una vida, un amor.
Nos cobijaban techos,
menos que techos, nubes;
menos que nubes, cielos;
aun menos, aire, nada.
Atravesando mares
hechos de veinte lágrimas,
diez tuyas y diez mías,
llegábamos a cuentas
doradas de collar,
islas limpias, desiertas,
sin flores y sin carne;
albergue, tan menudo,
en vidrio, de un amor
que se bastaba él solo
para el querer más grande
y no pedía auxilio
a los barcos ni al tiempo.

Not in palaces of marble,
not in months, no, nor in numbers,
never treading the ground:
in light, fragile worlds
we have lived together.
Time was scarcely
reckoned in minutes:
a minute was a century,
a life, a love.
Roofs used to shelter us;
less than roofs, clouds;
less than clouds, skies;
even less, air, nothing.
Crossing seas
made of twenty tears,
ten of yours and ten of mine,
we'd reach the golden
beads of a necklace,
limpid islands, deserted,
without flowers and without flesh;
shelter, so small,
made of glass, of a love
sufficient by itself
for the deepest loving,
and asking no help
from ships or from time.

Galerías enormes
abriendo
en los granos de arena,
descubrimos las minas
de llamas o de azares.
Y todo
colgando de aquel hilo
que sostenía, ¿quién?
Por eso nuestra vida
no parece vivida:
desliz, resbaladora,
ni estelas ni pisadas
dejó detrás. Si quieres
recordarla, no mires
donde se buscan siempre
las huellas y el recuerdo.
No te mires al alma,
a la sombra, a los labios.
Mírate bien la palma
de la mano, vacía.

Opening
enormous galleries
in the grains of sand,
we uncovered mines
of flames or of destinies.
And everything
hanging by that thread
held by whom?
That's why our life
appears unlived:
slipping, backsliding,
it left behind neither wakes
nor footprints. If you wish
to recall it, don't go looking
where traces and memories
are always searched for.
Don't look in your soul,
in your shadow, in your lips.
Look deep into the palm
of your hand, empty.

Pedro Salinas (1891–1951)
Chronological Outline of
His Life and Works

1891 27 November, born in Madrid

1909 Completes secondary education at the Instituto de San Isidro and begins to study at the University of Madrid, in both the Faculty of Letters and the Law Faculty

1913 Receives degree of licentiate at University of Madrid where he will also take the doctorate in 1915. He has already begun to write poetry, some poems published in *Prometeo*

Translates some poems from French for an anthology edited by Enrique Diez-Canedo

1914–17 At the Sorbonne, lecturer in Spanish. Paris for him, as for so many American writers is the "movable feast" Hemingway writes about; like them, he acquires there his love of art and his belief in the supreme value of poetry, all creative literature

1915 Marries Margarita Bonmatí, whose family came from Alicante and Algiers. The Mediterranean sea and light profoundly affect his vision of reality

1918 Named to chair in Spanish literature at University of Seville, after taking national competitive examination for
to university professors. Andalusia enchants him with its grace, elegance

1922–23 Lecturer at the University of Cambridge

1928 Transferred to University of Madrid; also teaches at the Centro de Estudios Históricos, with Ramón Menéndez Pidal and other very distinguished scholars of the time; during frequent sojourns in the capital, in the famous twenties, he is a friend of the leading writers: Unamuno,

Antonio Machado, Azorín, Valle-Inclán, Juan Ramón Jiménez, and the poets of his generation, particularly Jorge Guillén, and the younger poets, Lorca, etc.

1920   Translates Alfred de Musset, *Los caprichos de Mariana y otras comedias*
1922   Translates Marcel Proust, *A la sombra de las muchachas en flor*, 2 vols.
1923   *Presagios* (Madrid), first book of poems
1925   Edition and study of poetry of Meléndez Valdés
1926   *Víspera del gozo* (Madrid), fiction
1926–34   Translates into modern Spanish *Poema de mio cid* (Madrid)
1929   *Seguro azar* (Madrid), second book of poems
1931   *Fábula y signo* (Madrid), third book of poems
       Translation of Marcel Proust, *El mundo de Guermantes* (Madrid), in collaboration with J. M. Quiroga
1933   *La voz a ti debida* (Madrid), prepublication selection of poems from this book appeared under the title *amor en vilo* (Madrid)
       Edition and study of poetic work of San Juan de la Cruz (Madrid)
       Edition and study of *Maravilla del mundo* by Fray Luis de Granada (Madrid)
1932–36   Editor of literary review *Indice literario*, to which he contributes many articles and reviews; these are not listed separately here

1931–34   Summers, directs the International University of Santander
1936   Emigrates to United States; voluntary exile to 1951
1936–40   Professor at Wellesley College
1940–51   Professor at Johns Hopkins University, except for 1943–46, professor at the University of Puerto Rico, San Juan
       Lectures for ten summers at the Middlebury Spanish School

1940   *Reality and the Poet in Spanish Poetry* (Baltimore: The Johns Hopkins University Press), The Turnbull

lectures delivered in 1937; translated into English by
Edith Helman; new edition, 1966

1941 *Literatura española siglo XX* (Mexico)
1946 *El contemplado* (mar, poema) (Mexico)
1947 *Jorge Manrique: Tradición y originalidad* (Buenos
Aires)
1948 *La poesía de Ruben Darío* (Buenos Aires)
El defensor (Bogotá; reprinted Madrid: Alianza,
1967)
1949 *Todo más claro y otros poemas* (Buenos Aires)
1950 *La bomba increíble fabulación* (Buenos Aires)
1951 *El desnudo impecable y otras narraciones* (Mexico)

COLLECTED WORKS
1942 *Poesía junta* (Buenos Aires)

1951 Pedro Salinas died in Boston, after long illness, December 4

PUBLISHED POSTHUMOUSLY
1954 *Confianza* (Madrid)
1957 *Teatro completo* (Madrid)
1958 *Ensayos de literatura hispánica: Poema del Cid a
García Lorca* (Madrid)

COLLECTED WORKS
1955 *Poesías completas* (Madrid: Aguilar)
1971 *Poesías completas* (Barcelona: Barral), edited by
Soledad Salinas de Marichal; *Largo lamento*, written
probably from 1936 to 1938, was published in its most
complete form to date in this edition.

227

Índice de primeros versos

A continuación del primer verso de cada poema se indica su procedencia con arreglo a las abreviaciones siguientes: